Reading Between the Bones

Bones

The Pioneers of Dinosaur Paleontology

by Susan Clinton

Reading Between the Bones

The Pioneers of Dinosaur Paleontology

by

Susan Clinton

LIVES IN SCIENCE

Franklin Watts
A Division of Grolier Publishing
New York · London · Hong Kong · Sydney · Danbury, Connecticut

Interior Design and Page Make-up by Claire Fontaine

Photographs ©: Courtesy of Department of Library Services, American Museum of Natural History: cover center left (neg. #129039), cover backdrop (neg. #35383), 13 (neg. #31751), 20 (neg. #311184), 35 (neg. #38611), 45 (neg. #38991), 53 (neg. #35775), 60 (neg. #35805), 68 (neg. #258467), 71 (neg. #17837), 77 (neg. #410960); Archive Photos: 25; Corbis-Bettmann: 34, 41, 91, 99; Culver Pictures: 10, 29, 47, 49; Gamma-Liaison: cover top left (Patrick Aventurier), cover bottom left (Gleason); Museum of the Rockies: 105, 107, 110 (Bruce Selyem); Photo Researchers: 57 (Kenneth Fink), 63, 112 (Francois Gohier); Reuters/Corbis-Bettmann: 66; Smithsonian Institution: 55, 93; Superstock, Inc.: 89, 115; UPI/Corbis-Bettmann: 64, 75, 79.

Illustrations pp. 83, 95 by Scott Hartman, Tate Museum.

Library of Congress Cataloging-in-Publication Data
Clinton, Susan.
    Reading between the bones : the pioneers of dinosaur paleontology / by Susan Clinton.
        p. cm. — (Lives in science)
    Includes bibliographical references and index.
    Summary: Profiles eight of the people whose study of dinosaurs has shaped the field of paleontology over the past two hundred years.
    ISBN 0-531-11324-8
    1. Paleontologists — Biography — Juvenile literature. 2. Dinosaurs — Juvenile literature. [1. Paleontologists.] I. Title. II. Series.
    QE707.A2C57 1997
    560'.9
    [B]—DC20   96-36132
                                                CIP   AC

Contents

Introduction

This book profiles eight of the people who have brought us dinosaurs. Without their work—digging up bones in the field and studying them in the lab—we wouldn't know nearly as much as we do about these animals that ruled the world for 160 million years. The study of dinosaurs is a part of the science called vertebrate paleontology. It is a young science—only about 200 years old. Before then, people had no idea that dinosaurs had ever existed. It's also a fast-growing science. Since the first discovery of a dinosaur bone in 1824, paleontologists have identified more than 300 kinds of dinosaurs.

In some ways, the real subject of this book is how a scientific field grows—how knowledge builds. The profiles begin with Georges Cuvier, the founder of paleontology, and continue through Robert Bakker and John Horner, two of the leaders in the field at the close of the twentieth century. To some extent, the growth of dinosaur paleontology is cumulative; each of these scientists has given much thought and study to the work of those who preceded him. But in another sense, the growth of knowledge in this field, the play of ideas across decades, is anything but a smooth progression. Ideas are put forward and win acceptance only to be overturned by new evidence. Usually, the evidence consists of fossils, which are traces of prehistoric life that have hardened into stone and been preserved. Explanations based on fragmentary knowledge have to be put aside when new or more complete fossils come to light.

New fossils keep coming to light. The search for new fossils has always been a big part of dinosaur paleontology. All the people profiled here have made wonderful finds in the field. They also share something else—a loyalty to the bones. Every single person profiled here has been presented with fossils that no one had ever seen before. All of them are distinguished by the way they look at a new fossil; by the way they respect it as an irrefutable fact. Bones are the facts of paleontology. These people are pioneers of paleontology because they weren't afraid to demolish some accepted ideas when those ideas failed to explain the bones.

They also share a special kind of creative imagination, grounded in knowledge and common sense. Paleontologists need imagination. After all, dinosaurs are extinct. No one will ever be able to observe them in the wild. Since Cuvier's time, it has been an accepted practice to compare fossil animals to living ones, but which living ones? In the nineteenth century, Gideon Mantell thought of dinosaurs as fantastic lizards; now, more and more paleontologists believe that birds are the direct descendants of dinosaurs. Understanding dinosaurs and their behavior requires great patience in assembling evidence and great ingenuity in interpreting it.

Working in a field where there can be no living proof means you risk being wrong—assuming something you should have questioned; drawing conclusions with too little data; forgetting to take some crucial factor into account. New ideas about dinosaurs usually create plenty of controversy. Every one of the figures profiled here has made discoveries or contributed ideas that have changed the course of paleontology. Every one of them has drawn opponents that believe he's out-and-out wrong. And once in a while, it is heartening to know, they have been wrong. Sometimes the mistake is in the details, as when Gideon Mantell mounted the iguanodon's thumb spur on its nose. Sometimes the mistake is in a major assumption. Georges Cuvier, for example, founded much of his work on the idea that animal species do not change. After Cuvier's death, Charles Darwin's theory of evolution put forth the opposite idea: that species undergo constant change and that, over time, new species evolve from older ones. Cuvier was wrong, but the value of his work stands.

Dinosaur paleontology is not an easy profession to live with. It requires years of education and the freedom to go out collecting fossils for months at a time. Until fairly recently, women's roles have not left them the freedom or flexibility to take up paleontology. A few women's names appear in earlier times; for example, in nineteenth-century England, a woman named Mary Anning was a well-known fossil collector. In modern times, women's names have begun to appear as expedition leaders and specialists in different branches of paleontology. But it is still true that the best known, most influential, and most controversial people in the field are men.

Shaping a career in dinosaur paleontology requires its share of ingenuity. Most of the people profiled here allied themselves with major cultural institutions, such as universities and museums. Some were wealthy enough to fund their own work. Several have become science celebrities. All of them have sought to attract public interest and support by planning exhibits or giving lectures or writing books. Dinosaurs are unfailingly interesting to them and they want the public to feel the same way. These people love what they do, and they will go out on a limb to do it, even if it frequently requires a hot, dusty, desert dig. When they don't find what they expected to find where they expected to find it, they have the courage and patience to start over and look at what turns up. That's loyalty to the bones.

Georges Cuvier

"A Lizard of the Size of a Whale"

Georges Cuvier and the Discovery of Extinction

Early in the nineteenth century, a French anatomist named Georges Cuvier made a bold claim. Give him a bone, any bone, Cuvier offered, and he would describe the animal it came from. Given one sharp tooth, Cuvier could fill in the rest—the jawline; the neck, shoulder, and leg muscles; the claws; the strength and speed of the animal's pounce; the sharpness of its senses; even the arrangement of its digestive tract. Sometimes he seemed more like a magician than a scientist. No one, scientists agreed, had ever understood anatomy as thoroughly as Georges Cuvier.

Then someone brought him a fossil bone.

In Cuvier's time, science hadn't yet begun to understand the long history of life on earth. People could not go to museums to see skeletons of prehistoric beasts. No one knew there were any prehistoric beasts. Not a single dinosaur had been identified; the word "dinosaur" hadn't been coined yet. Fossil bones and shells turned up from time to time, dug up by farmers, along seaside cliffs, or in stone quarries, but there were as yet no complete skeletons, and none of the truly gigantic bones had come to light. People knew that fossils were odd, but they did not know how odd. They did not know what prehistoric animals looked like—until someone asked Georges Cuvier.

When he was presented with fossil bones, Cuvier was not daunted. He simply proceeded to describe animals that no one had ever seen. He presented one amazing creature after another: a flying reptile; a tapir-like animal as big as a horse; a sloth the size of a rhinoceros. Today we know these animals by the names he gave them—pterodactyl, paleotherium, and megatherium. These animals looked like the products of fantasy or magic, but they weren't; they were products of science.

Out of Cuvier's fossil studies grew the science of paleontology, which is rooted in the study of animal anatomy. Cuvier began his work in paleontology in 1796 with a controversial study of elephant bones. He compared elephant skeletons from Africa and India with some fossil bones from two unlikely locations: Russian Siberia and the Ohio River Valley in North America. The big fossil jaws and tusks looked like elephant bones, but what were they doing in places like Ohio and Siberia, where no one had ever seen a living elephant?

Many Americans imagined that herds of these big animals had simply moved on to the unexplored West. Siberian folklore held that these were the bones of a big underground animal, like a giant mole, that burrowed around unseen. Cuvier disagreed. First, Cuvier noted, the fossil bones belonged to two new species, the mammoth (Siberia) and the mastodon (America). Second, no one had ever seen a living mammoth or mastodon, not because they burrowed underground and not because they roamed out West, but because there weren't any. All of them had died out; they were extinct.

Declaring that any kind of animal had died out was shocking. Many people, even in the scientific world, saw the concept of extinction as an affront to religion. Most Europeans of Cuvier's time believed that God had created the

Backed by fossil evidence such as this mastodon skeleton, Cuvier
silenced those who at first did not believe extinction possible.

earth perfect and unchanging from the beginning of time.
When Cuvier pronounced the mammoths and mastodons
extinct, he raised troubling questions. After all, why would
God allow one of His designs to die out? But nobody could
ignore Cuvier's fossil evidence. Mammoths and mastodons
were very large land animals. If they had been sea creatures,
maybe, just maybe, they could live concealed in the deep

ocean. But if land animals the size of mammoths were tramping around, people would have known about it.

Cuvier did not want to attack belief in God as Creator. He was a religious man. But he wanted people to recognize that life on earth had not been static and unchanging. Fossils proved it. The earth had a history, life had a history, and extinction was the key to unraveling it.

When Cuvier first presented his ideas, French scientists were impressed, but not convinced. Who was this young scientist and how could he speak with such certainty?

Georges Cuvier was brilliant and ambitious, intense and hardworking. Ever since he was a child, Cuvier had taken life seriously. He had to. From an early age Cuvier understood that his family's future rested firmly on his shoulders. He was born on August 23, 1769, the second child of a retired soldier and his young wife. The couple's first son had died at the age of four, a few months before Georges was born. Although he was named Jean-Léopold-Nicolas-Frédéric-Dagobert, the young Cuvier was always called Georges after his dead brother.

The Cuvier family lived in the town of Montbéliard in a region called Alsace. During Cuvier's childhood, Alsace was part of the German kingdom of Württemberg. Later it was taken over by France. Germany at the time was largely Protestant and so were most people in Montbéliard. The language of Montbéliard, however, was French. Cuvier's family depended on a military pension his father received from the French government. As the French monarchy struggled under debt, the pension came less and less regularly.

Georges was a weak, sickly, but clearly very bright child. His mother watched over him carefully, taught him to read by age four, and hired an architect to teach him drawing. When he went to school, Cuvier excelled. A classmate remembered him as a pale, thin twelve-year-old who didn't allow himself to join in the other boys' games. Cuvier's parents had been counting on him to win a place in a free school where young men trained to be ministers. But one teacher ranked him too low to qualify, and he missed his chance. For the Cuvier family, this was a disaster. They could not afford any further education for their son. Fortunately, Georges came to the attention of a local nobleman, who decided to pay Georges's way to the Karlsschule, a school founded to train administrators.

The Karlsschule was in Stuttgart, Germany, a three-day carriage trip from Cuvier's home. It was a military school where students wore uniforms, lived in barracks, and followed a strictly regimented schedule. Cuvier had never been away from home. For the rest of his life, he remembered how frightened he was on the trip to Stuttgart. He sat in a carriage between two officials who rattled on in German the entire trip. Cuvier couldn't understand a word. He would have to learn fast; all the classes at the Karlsschule were taught in German.

In 1788, Cuvier graduated from the Karlsschule as one of its top students with an excellent chance for a government post. The problem was that there were no posts open, even for the brightest. Meanwhile, the French Revolution had begun, leaving France in turmoil and ending his family's pension. Cuvier couldn't wait for a post to open up; he had to earn some money. When a wealthy French family offered him a job tutoring their son, Cuvier accepted, even though this post was far beneath his training and his ambitions. Instead of an administrator, he was now just a notch above a servant.

The family lived in Normandy, a region on the northwest coast of France. Here Cuvier was far from any centers of culture or learning. But he was also far from the danger and turmoil of the French Revolution. During the Revolution, the common people of France rose up against the king and nobility. They fought to end the power of the privileged class and establish social equality. The king and many members of the nobility were beheaded to make way for the new order. Scientific work, which had been funded by the king, came under suspicion, and many intellectuals and men of science fled France or went into hiding. Some were beheaded.

Cuvier spent these tumultuous years in the Norman countryside with lots of time on his hands. He took up the study of animal life with a new seriousness and dedication. He began systematically dissecting, drawing, and describing different groups of animals, starting with the mollusks he found along the seashore. As he became more involved in this work, Cuvier began exchanging letters with French men of science and making his work known.

When Cuvier dissected an animal, whether it was a mollusk or a beetle or a cat, he wanted to know how its internal organs worked and how they were linked together in systems. How did the animal digest food? What made it move? How did it perceive the outside world? In the late eighteenth century, Cuvier's work was new. Naturalists before Cuvier had studied a few animals, but no study included the range of creatures or the level of detail that distinguished Cuvier's research.

Although Cuvier could do solid scientific work in provincial Normandy, only in Paris would he be able to make a career of it. By 1795, the days of mob rule and daily beheadings were ending. The new government tried to reorganize French institutions to reflect the ideal of equality. With this in mind, the former Royal Cabinet was turned into a public institution, the National Museum of Natural History.

Since the Renaissance, royal households had kept curio cabinets filled with interesting objects such as rocks and shells, pressed plants, mounted insects, and animal specimens. Even though some of these collections eventually grew out of their cupboards to fill whole buildings, the word "cabinet" stuck. When the Royal Cabinet became the Museum of Natural History, it included a zoo, a botanical garden, a library, and entire buildings full of specimens. The museum was to be staffed by twelve professors whose main job was to give public lectures. Cuvier wanted one of these jobs.

Before the Revolution, he wouldn't have had much of a chance: he was a commoner, not a nobleman; he had no wealth; he was Protestant in a Catholic country; and he was a provincial outsider to the political and social life of the capital. However, in 1795, everything was in flux. Many leading scientists had fled or been executed. Old schools and institutions had been closed; new ones formed. His letter-writing had won Cuvier some influential friends. Cuvier was also lucky. The museum's professor of animal anatomy was too old to give lectures; he hired Cuvier as his substitute.

With the job came a place to live. Professors and many of their assistants lived in the museum's compound of buildings. Cuvier moved in and stayed for the rest of his life. At first, he shared an apartment. A few years later, he was given his own house. Finally, Cuvier had workmen build a passage from his second floor directly into the mollusk room of the comparative anatomy building.

When Cuvier started, the museum had just bought a group of buildings formerly used as carriage garages. Cuvier got to work filling one of these buildings with anatomy exhibits. He hunted in the attic for jumbled skeletons, dusted them off, and reassembled them for display. He wrote to scientists and explorers asking them to send him new specimens. If one of the museum's zoo animals died, Cuvier took it off to his lab to dissect. Some mornings visitors would catch sight of Cuvier taking a break, strolling the grounds in his bloody dissecting jacket.

In the press of his work, Cuvier's ideas about the classification of animals took shape. He began with the assumption that each animal could only be understood as a whole, that its systems—of digestion, or perception, or reproduction—all worked together to fit the animal for its environment. He called this the principle of the correlation of parts. Cuvier wrote, "A bird is a bird in all and every part; it is the same with a fish or an insect." By means of this principle, "Each species may be determined, with perfect certainty, by any fragment of any of its parts."

To understand how animals were related to one another, Cuvier compared their various organs and systems. When his exhibit hall, the Cabinet of Comparative Anatomy, opened to the public in 1806, the exhibits were arranged as a comparative anatomy lesson. Because teeth were useful in classifying mammals, one of the galleries contained only mammal teeth—870 of them, ranging from the tusks of a walrus to the incisors of a bat. In another room, Cuvier had arranged 300 sets of cranial (skull) bones of various animals, including humans. In other rooms, jars of alcohol preserved animals' brains, hearts, muscles, and eyes.

The museum soon assembled the best collection of animal specimens in the world. In 1817, Cuvier published a huge work, *Le Règne animal distribué d'après son organisation* (*The Animal Kingdom, Distributed According to its Organization*), which classified and described almost every known animal. Cuvier's approach to studying animals, presented in his lectures, his books, and his exhibition halls, established comparative anatomy as a new branch of science.

The working conditions at the museum made it possible for Cuvier to produce his massive published works. A visiting geologist, Charles Lyell, called Cuvier's writing studio his "sanctum sanctorum," meaning "holy of holies." Lyell described the studio as a long, well-lit, quiet room with eleven desks, made for the author to work standing up. Each desk was a complete work station for a different book, or part of a book, with its own pens and paper, notes, completed pages, and research materials. Cuvier moved from desk to desk, working on different projects, adding a section here, a section there. Lyell writes, "It is truly characteristic of the man. In every part, it displays that extraordinary power of methodizing which is the grand secret of the prodigious feats which he performs annually without appearing to give himself the least trouble."

Cuvier's vast experience in comparative anatomy helped him solve problems with fossil reconstructions. For example, some fossil bones from a quarry at Montmartre near Paris raised a difficult question. The quarry yielded two sets of teeth and two sets of foot bones, but which feet went with which teeth? From the teeth and other associated bones, Cuvier identified two animals: *Paleotherium*, a large animal with a snout like a tapir's, and *Anoplotherium*, an otter-like animal with a smaller, oblong head.

One fossil foot was small and three-toed; the other was larger and two-toed. Cuvier knew that the larger foot would not necessarily match the larger head. In the end, he used two facts to make the match. First, the small, three-toed feet were more abundant than the two-toed ones and probably went with the more abundant *Paleotherium* teeth. Secondly, the animal the *Paleotherium* most resembled, the tapir, has three-toed back feet. That settled it. Cuvier assigned the small, three-toed feet to *Paleotherium* and the longer, two-toed ones to *Anoplotherium*. He wrote, "No naturalist habituated to the analogies which are so constant in all organized creatures can restrain himself from spontaneously crying out that this foot is made for this head and this head for this foot."

Although the museum's resources were wonderful, Cuvier found the pay meager. His need became more pressing when he married Anne-Marie Coquet de Trayzaile in 1803. Cuvier's wife was a widow; her first husband, Philippe Duvaucel had been executed during the Revolution, leaving her with four children and no fortune. Cuvier and his wife

When Cuvier first described prehistoric creatures, such as the pterodactyl captured in this fossil belonging to the American Museum of Natural History, they sounded more like the products of a creative imagination than the findings of a meticulous scientist.

had four more children together. Sadly, none of Cuvier's own children survived him. The couple's first son died as an infant; their four-year-old daughter died in 1812; their seven-year-old son in 1813. The hardest loss was the death of his twenty-two-year-old daughter Clementine on September 28, 1828.

In addition to his job at the museum, Cuvier held other teaching and administrative posts. He was one of the best known and most successful public men of his time. Cuvier was not a modest man; he worked constantly to bring his accomplishments to the attention of people in power. The most prestigious group of scientists in France was the Institute des Sciences. Seeking to supplement his income, Cuvier managed to win a lifelong appointment as its secretary. His duties were to deliver eulogies on members who had died and to report to the emperor, Napoleon (in later years, to the king), on scientific developments. Besides coming with a substantial salary, this position gave him power over the reputation and advancement of others.

In 1812, Napoleon named him to the Council of State, a policy-setting group that reported to the emperor. Cuvier's special field on the council was education. He advocated education for the poor and fought to keep higher education out of the control of religious orders. Cuvier remained on the Council of State all through the political ups and downs of the next twenty years. Napoleon was overthrown; kings were restored. Five different regimes came and went as Cuvier accumulated more appointments, more power, and more honors.

His increasing power made him a very influential man, if not a very popular one. His manner at official functions was stiff and severe. Like many very busy people, Cuvier was irritable and impatient. He hated to be kept waiting and pestered anyone working for him until a project was complete. Cuvier took his honors seriously. He designed ceremonial robes for a national university including a purple velvet robe bordered with ermine for himself. The coats he wore for formal functions were covered with the various ribbons and medals he had been awarded. Some people accused him of piling up appointments for the sole purpose of adding to his income. Others questioned how he could get along with so many different rulers.

Cuvier was not simply a title-seeker. He worked hard at his administrative posts to the point where these responsibilities crowded out his scientific work. If any theme runs through Cuvier's work, it is the love of order. As a scientist, he sought principles that would order the diversity of the animal kingdom. As an administrator, he supported any government that could bring order to society. As a thinker, he distrusted speculation; he put all his faith in facts.

When Cuvier was sure of his facts, he brought all his power to bear to win his point. He could distribute teaching posts to those that agreed with him and deny them to his intellectual opponents. He could make sure that some research papers received favorable attention while others were criticized or dismissed. His annual reports on the state of scientific research could single out those he felt were doing important work and omit others. When he was right, as he was about extinction, Cuvier's authority could speed the pace of scientific advances. But sometimes, Cuvier was wrong.

As he inspected fossil-bearing sites around Paris, Cuvier realized that different layers of rock contained different kinds of fossils. Moreover, the deeper the rock bed, the stranger the creatures, that is, the more unlike any living animals. Why should this be so? Why did more recent extinct animals have a stronger resemblance to living ones? Why did simpler life forms appear earlier and more complex ones later in the fossil record?

One of Cuvier's colleagues and rivals, Étienne Geoffroy

Saint-Hilaire believed that the fossil record showed that complex animals somehow developed from simpler ones. He put forward the idea that there was an underlying unity through the whole animal kingdom. Geoffroy knew he didn't have enough evidence to prove his point, but he declared that it was "the right and property of genius" to go beyond the facts in order to reach great truths.

All his life, Cuvier had insisted on sticking to the facts. Moreover, the suggestion that one kind of animal could change into another kind went against all Cuvier's most strongly held ideas. For him, each species had to be permanently fixed, for if all the parts of an animal must work together for its survival, how can any part change?

Cuvier concluded that the change from one animal population to another had not been gradual, but sudden and catastrophic. Entire populations must have been wiped out by some natural disaster—flooding or volcanoes—to be replaced by new animals that migrated in. For Cuvier, past eras were as separate as were species. He wrote, "There is nothing that could in the slightest degree, give support to the opinion that the new genera which I have discovered or established among the fossil remains of animals . . . might have been the sources of the present race of animals."

Besides, Cuvier argued, if these changes had occurred, wouldn't there be fossils of the changing forms? To prove his point, Cuvier examined the mummified remains of animals brought to Paris by Napoleon's Egyptian expedition. He found that these three-thousand-year-old cats and ibises were identical to the modern animals. If gradual change were possible, he argued, wouldn't it have happened in three thousand years?

In 1859, about thirty years after Cuvier's death, Charles Darwin would publish his theory of evolution and natural selection. Where Cuvier saw a fixed and unalterable relationship between animal and environment, Darwin saw a continuous process of adaptation and natural selection. Darwin observed that animal species do change. Some of these changes, or adaptations, make individual animals more likely to survive and produce more offspring. Over time, the population of these better adapted animals increases.

By the 1880s, fossil beds in North America would yield the evidence that was missing in Cuvier's time. Yale paleontologist O. C. Marsh would assemble a series of prehistoric horses that clearly showed the gradual evolution of this lineage over time. In fact, fossil evidence would become one of the main supports for the theory of evolution. However, the time scale for these changes greatly exceeded that imagined by Cuvier or his contemporaries. The time needed for these changes would be measured not in thousands of years but in millions.

In 1830, Cuvier publicly debated Geoffroy Saint-Hilaire. Geoffroy argued for unity of structure throughout the animal kingdom, Cuvier for the permanent separation of species. Cuvier attacked with his usual lucid, logical command of fact and demolished Geoffroy's more nebulous ideas. Scientists and learned men all over Europe followed the debate. Cuvier was seen as a spokesman for conservative, entrenched authority. Geoffroy was taken as a representative of new and daring ideas. Although Cuvier's clear victory in the debating hall fortified his views in Paris, he could not silence questions that naturally arose from any thoughtful overview of the animal world.

Cuvier had made that overview possible. He had imposed order on an animal world of amazing variety and diversity. His firm defense of the idea of extinction had opened the door to the study of the earth's past. As a scientist and a public man, Cuvier was incredibly productive and successful. But the very ideas and drive for order that led to his great advances kept him from pursuing the questions raised by his own work.

Cuvier lecturing in 1830

On Tuesday, May 8, 1832, Cuvier lectured on the history of science to an overflowing crowd. That evening, his right arm was numb. The next day, he could not swallow. Cuvier knew that he was dying, and he knew that nothing could be done about it. On Saturday, he told a friend, "I had great things still to do. All was ready in my head; after thirty years of labour and research, there remained but to write; and now the hands fail, and carry with them the head." Cuvier died on Sunday afternoon, May 13, 1832.

Fortunately, Cuvier had published his work on paleontology in a book called *Discours sur les révolutions de la surface du globe*. The English translator, Robert Jameson, gave it the title *Essay on the Theory of the Earth*. The book gathers together Cuvier's clear, precise descriptions of fossil animals. Some of the animals Cuvier discovered himself; others were specimens sent to him for identification. One unusual specimen, found in England by a Professor William Buckland, is identified by Cuvier as a reptile, much like a monitor lizard. But, he writes, "If we suppose it to have possessed the proportions of the monitors, it must have exceeded seventy feet in length. It was, in fact, a lizard of the size of a whale."

Once again, Cuvier had made good on his boast. From a few bones, he was able to envision an animal the likes of which no one had ever seen. When Cuvier came to this conclusion, no one had heard of dinosaurs; the word would not be coined until 1841. But Cuvier had laid the groundwork for the spectacular dinosaur discoveries to come. The whale-sized lizard Cuvier envisioned was the first dinosaur ever described. Buckland published the description in 1824. He named it, in Cuvier's honor, *Megalosaurus cuvieri*, Cuvier's great fossil lizard.

2

"In the Midst of Wonders"
Gideon Mantell and the Newfound Age of Reptiles

Gideon Algernon Mantell, a nineteenth-century English country doctor, had a passion for fossils. As he walked down lanes making calls, Mantell kept a sharp eye on the loose piles of rock lining the road. When he drove his carriage around the countryside visiting patients, Mantell stopped to look at stony outcroppings and talk with quarry workers. People in Mantell's part of England, the southwestern county of Sussex, were used to seeing fossils. But no one else in Mantell's town of Lewes collected as many and studied them as seriously.

Only an experienced fossil collector like Mantell would have been able to envision an extraordinary new animal on the evidence of a single fossil tooth. Mantell had the experience, the determination, and the vision to introduce the world to *Iguanodon*, the first known herbivorous dinosaur. Mantell made other significant discoveries in paleontology and geology; in fact, three of the earliest known dinosaurs were first identified and described by him. Yet, despite his original and important contributions, Mantell never had the opportunity to make paleontology his profession.

In early nineteenth-century England, fossil hunting was a fashionable thing to do. Amateur enthusiasts went on collecting excursions. People flocked to public lectures about geology and paleontology. Interest in this "young" science was widespread, but very few professional positions existed. Most serious work in geology and paleontology was being done by wealthy men who had the leisure and the money to follow their interests. These men formed private scientific societies, such as the Geological Society, to publish their discoveries and discuss their ideas. These societies were not open to just any interested person; members had to be elected by the group and pay hefty annual dues.

Mantell was elected to the scientific societies, but unlike many of the other members, he had to work to support himself and his family. All his life, he struggled to find the time and energy for his fossils. It was a strain on his health, his finances, and his family. Mantell's life was literally crowded with fossils. His home became a kind of museum, and his nights were given over to drawing and describing fossils.

Mantell's fascination with fossils began during his boyhood in Lewes. Mantell was born there on February 3, 1790. He grew up in a very pious household with three brothers and three sisters. His father, Thomas Mantell, was a shoemaker, but the Mantell family had once been a knightly family. One ancestor had gone crusading with Richard I. As an adult, Gideon Mantell made the most of his family's history by displaying the Mantell coat-of-arms on his carriage.

Lewes was a small town surrounded by ruins and traces of the past: Roman tombs, a medieval castle, a ruined monastery. Mantell, however, paid the most attention to remains of a different kind—the chalky limestone of Sussex that preserved fossils from an ancient sea. One of these marine fossils was Mantell's first memorable find. He and a friend were trekking along a streambank when he noticed an unusual rock. After the two boys dragged it out of the water and contemplated it, Gideon pronounced the rock a fossil because he remembered seeing a magazine picture of such a thing. He was correct. He had found the spiral shell of an ammonite.

Gideon Mantell

Nobody in town could teach him about geology, but Mantell learned as much as he could from the science books in the town's library. Equipped with this knowledge, Mantell discovered that the fossils in a nearby rock layer belonged not to marine animals, but to terrestrial animals. This rock layer of Cretaceous clays and sandstones was called the Wealden. The Wealden would be the source of Mantell's greatest fossil discoveries.

As a shoemaker's son, Mantell had to find some way to make a living. In his teens, he started working as an apprentice to a Lewes doctor named James Moore. This meant he went on calls with Moore, observing, helping when he could, and learning medicine on the spot. For several years, Mantell went to London to study medicine at St. Bartholomew's Hospital. By 1816, he was back in Lewes practicing medicine as Moore's partner.

As Mantell settled into his practice in Lewes, he also moved into Castle Place, the house where he would live for the next twenty years. On May 4, 1816, he married the daughter of one of his patients, Mary Ann Woodhouse. Their first child, Ellen, was born in 1818, followed by Walter in 1820, Hannah in 1822, and Reginald in 1827. Mantell seems to have been very successful as a medical man. His training in London gave him prestige. His association with Moore introduced him to patients. On a slow day, he would visit thirty patients, sixty on a busy day. Mantell was well on his way to becoming one of Lewes's leading citizens. The Mantells were often seen at dinner parties and the theater. They kept a cook. As Mantell wrote, he liked his house to be "neat and tasty." His spotless carriage and groom waited at the door, ready to take him out on calls.

Throughout this busy period of establishing his career and starting his family, Mantell also devoted time to what he called the "organic remains of a former world." He claimed to have developed the habit of allowing himself only four hours of sleep a night. In 1822, he published a 300-page book, *The Fossils of the South Downs*, illustrated with his own drawings of 364 fossils.

Mary Ann Mantell also contributed to this first book. She learned lithography, and over a period of four years, she engraved plates for the printing of all the illustrations. Mantell acknowledges her work in words that show how proud he was of her and how demanding he must have been of himself and others, "As the engravings are the first performance of a lady but little skilled in the art, I am most anxious to claim for them every indulgence. I am well aware that the partiality of a husband may render me insensible to their defects; but, although they may be destitute of that neatness and uniformity which distinguish the works of the professed artist, they will not, I trust, be found deficient in the more essential requisite of correctness."

That same year, Mary Ann Mantell made another important contribution to Mantell's study of fossils. She found a large fossil tooth with a worn, flattened crown. Because of her work on the book plates, it is certain that Mary Ann Mantell was very familiar with the known fossils of the region. This was not one she had seen before. The pattern of wear seemed to show that the tooth belonged to a plant-eating creature. The single root of the tooth resembled that of a reptile. But finding these two characteristics together puzzled Gideon Mantell. All known reptiles were carnivores, and none of them was able to chew.

Mantell took this puzzling fossil to a meeting of the Geological Society. There he showed it to some of the great men of science of his day. Mantell hoped this learned audience would agree with his hunch about this extraordinary tooth. He was disappointed. Someone suggested that the tooth belonged to a wolf-fish. Someone else thought it was a comparatively recent mammal fossil. Mantell rode home discouraged, but he didn't give up. Instead, he sent the tooth to a higher authority, Georges Cuvier at the Museum of Natural History in Paris. In the 1820s, Cuvier was well-established as an international authority on paleontology. Mantell placed a very high value on Cuvier's opinion, so he was extremely disappointed when Cuvier suggested his fossil could be a rhinoceros tooth.

By this time, Mantell had more bones to puzzle over. He had alerted quarrymen to be on the lookout for new fossils, and they had come through with more of the strange teeth, some bones from a huge forefoot, and a horn. Some of the new teeth were not so worn as the first one. They had what Mantell called a prismatic shape with serrated edges. The more Mantell pondered his growing collection of mystery fossils the more certain he became that these could not be the bones of a rhino or any other mammal. Mammal fossils simply were not found in this particular rock layer. It preserved a much more ancient world of tropical ferns and giant reptiles—crocodiles, turtles, and this mystery creature.

Mantell took his fossils back to London to the anatomy collection at the Hunterian Museum. There Mantell searched drawer after drawer of reptile bones looking for anything that resembled the fossil teeth. Finally a young man who was working at the museum took a look at Mantell's fossils. He led Mantell to the skeleton he had been working on, that of a Central American iguana. Here was the match. The iguana teeth were much smaller than the fossil's teeth, but they had the same shape. Mantell was now satisfied that his big herbivore was indeed a reptile.

In 1825, Mantell published a description of this new fossil animal, "Notice on the *Iguanodon*, a newly-discovered Fossil Reptile." Mantell had discovered the first known herbivorous dinosaur. He didn't call it a dinosaur; the word did not yet exist. In fact, he envisioned the *Iguanodon* as a kind of giant lizard, sprawling on all fours with a horn on its nose. (More complete information has since changed our view of the *Iguanodon* and of dinosaurs. Complete *Iguanodon* skeletons show that the "horn" is actually a spur on the dinosaur's thumb.)

Mantell's paper created quite a stir. The year it was published, Mantell was elected a member of the Royal Society, England's oldest and most prestigious scientific society. Perhaps even more gratifying, Cuvier studied the additional fossil teeth and changed his mind. The worn condition of the first tooth had deceived him. Cuvier now pronounced Mantell's fossils "geological treasures" and credited him with the discovery of a new animal.

Mantell returned to collecting with new zeal. The front room of his house at Castle Place gradually filled with display cases holding the *Iguanodon* bones and other fossils, as well as seventy models sent by Cuvier. In 1829, Mantell printed up a catalog of his collection, now officially called the Mantellian Museum. It was open to visitors by appointment on the first and third Tuesday of every month. Mantell didn't insist on this strict schedule of appointments, as he wrote to a friend, "my regulations are *daily* infringed upon to the great annoyance of Mrs. Mantell and the discomposure of my domestic arrangements."

As Mantell struggled to maintain his medical practice and his work with fossils his health began to suffer. He complained about the hardships of a country practice: interrupted rest, hours spent jolting along in carriages or on horseback, bending over the bedsides of the sick, and assisting births. The life of a country doctor left his back sore and aching. Sometimes he reported feeling more like a patient than a doctor.

In 1832, Mantell found the time to labor over a new find. Some quarrymen had been blasting out rock when they noticed fossil pieces in the fragments. They set them aside for Mantell. He sifted through and gathered fifty pieces of fossil-bearing rubble. Back home, "with much difficulty and

In the image above, an iguanodon (left) battles a megalosaur (right). This image reflects Mantell's vision of the iguanodon as an enormous, sprawling lizard with a horn on its nose. Later restorations such as the one on the opposite page show that the "horn" was actually the dinosaur's thumb spur. The most modern revisions show the iguanodon walking less erect, with its spine and tail almost parallel to the ground.

great labour" he cemented together the pieces to make a 5 by 3 foot (1.5 by 0.9 m) rock slab. Then Mantell began chiseling. Sometimes as the rock flaked apart, it shattered the fossils. Then he would collect every piece, glue the bone together, give it a few days to dry, and go back to chiseling.

The reward for all this exacting work was finding the remains of a new dinosaur. This animal had circular bony plates, called scutes, linked in long lines down its back, and sharp, flat spines, from 3 to 17 inches (7.6 to 43.2 cm) long,

standing in a crest down the middle of its back. He named it *Hylaeosaurus*, which means Wealden lizard. Mantell had described the first known armored dinosaur.

In 1833, Mantell moved his family to the seaside resort town of Brighton. The royal family sometimes summered in Brighton, and, as a result, it attracted an aristocratic population. Mantell was hoping for a more fashionable practice with wealthier patients and less traveling. He was also hoping for more recognition, perhaps royal recognition, for his scientific work.

Moving to Brighton was costly, especially because Mantell had new display cases made for his museum. The museum now filled an entire floor of the family's house. Mantell planned to recover the cost by charging admission, but his friends discouraged him. They felt it would damage his reputation as a doctor and a scientist. A doctor shouldn't be running a public entertainment, and a gentleman pursued science for its own sake. Mantell introduced himself to Brighton society by giving free lectures on geology; the lectures drew great crowds and made him, as he reports, "the Lion of the season." His museum at Brighton attracted hundreds of people—1,500 in the first six months—but only two or three of them became patients.

In the 1830s, Mantell had three children away at school and a house and servants to maintain. His scientific accomplishments had brought him into privileged circles, but he was hard pressed to support himself. In part because of his difficult position, he hungered for recognition and nursed a growing sense of being overlooked. He began to suffer from a nervous ailment, tic douloureux, or muscle spasms of the face.

Every time Mantell vowed to give up on his fossils and concentrate on medicine, a new discovery enticed him back. In 1834, a group of large fossil bones were found in a quarry near Maidstone, forty miles from Brighton. Mantell visited the quarry and recognized *Iguanodon* bones. This skeleton was more complete than anything Mantell had yet seen. It included parts of the back legs and large hind feet.

Mantell's paper on these bones earned him the Wollaston Medal of the Geological Society, but his growing fame was not attracting patients. Mantell couldn't give up his collection but he could no longer afford it either. He arranged to rent the museum to the local scientific society. Of course, this meant that the Mantells had to move out of the house.

Mantell rented rooms down the street for himself, but he sent his wife and children back to Lewes to live in a rented cottage.

Separated from his family and in need of income, Mantell made a painful decision. He would have to sell his paleontology collection and use the money to set himself up in a London medical practice. The British Museum agreed to buy the Mantellian Museum collection for four thousand pounds, more than enough to purchase a practice in London. In 1838, Mantell paid a last visit to his former home to look over his thousands of rocks and fossils. It was a painful visit. Mantell wrote, "Although my collection, the result of so much labour and toil, is lost to me for ever, yet I do feel, and proudly feel, that I have not lived in vain. . . . Other minds will be taught by my example to pursue under difficulties and trials the way of truth and knowledge."

Mantell had hoped that his collection would be kept together at the museum, but he was disappointed to see it broken up. Occasionally, Mantell went to see his fossils—once he reports rearranging the *Iguanodon* case. On another visit, he was very distressed to find a *Hylaeosaurus* femur shattered on the ground. "I picked it up and delivered it to an attendant! Such is the scandalous manner in which the national collection is neglected. This bone is unique and cost me several nights labor to extricate it from the stone!"

Mantell's medical practice in London was very busy. There would have been plenty of work for his sons to join the practice, but neither of his boys chose medicine as a career. Walter, the oldest, decided to seek his fortune in New Zealand and sailed away in 1839. While Mantell was negotiating to sell his museum, his fourteen-year-old daughter, Hannah, had contracted tuberculosis. The disease attacked her hip joint, leaving her unable to walk. In March 1840, Hannah died. Her death was a crushing blow to Mantell who had nursed her himself and often admired the sweet and patient way she endured her illness. Around this time, Mrs. Mantell left her husband. There was no divorce; the couple simply never lived together again. Mantell wrote to a friend, "There was a time when my poor wife felt deep interest in my pursuits, and was proud of my success, but of late years that feeling had passed away, and she was annoyed rather than gratified by my devotion to science."

No matter how many times Mantell proclaimed his farewell to science, he was never really willing to give it up. Little by little his London house began to fill up with new fossils and rock samples. Microscopes became "all the rage" in the early 1840s, and this new way of studying fossils delighted Mantell. His later books showed microscopic cross sections of *Iguanodon* teeth and *Hylaeosaurus* scutes. Moreover, living in London allowed Mantell to attend society meetings and the round of parties and receptions that welcomed men of science. At one dinner party, the guests took turns viewing one another's blood under a microscope. Mantell had slower circulation and larger corpuscles than the others, which made one guest joke that Mantell was after all part reptile!

At a time when everyone traveled on horses and in carriages, accidents were fairly common. Mantell had tended patients hurt in falls, trampled by horses, or crushed by wagons. In October 1841, the reins of Mantell's carriage got tangled. He fell, was dragged along the ground, and narrowly missed being crushed. A few days later, he found that his legs were paralyzed. The paralysis slowly diminished, but for the rest of his life, Mantell suffered terrible back pain. Gradually Mantell developed a hard swelling on his lower back. The doctors prescribed rest.

Mantell did not follow their advice. For the remaining eleven years of his life, he continued to visit patients, give lectures, make geological excursions, and participate in Geological Society meetings. In his diary and his letters he records the cost, in suffering, of every effort. Much of the time, any writing had to be done while he lay flat on his back, but this did not stop him from producing new books.

Mantell's daughter Ellen was now working on some drawings for him. Mantell apparently remained as demanding as ever, "The drawings . . . are very troublesome, for . . . they are obliged to be very small, and yet faithful; and you know unless they are also artistical my fastidious taste would not be satisfied." Ellen and her father must have quarreled because she left his home in 1844, and the two never met again. When his youngest son, Reginald, sailed to America to look for work building railroads, Mantell was left alone. He wrote to a friend, "My destiny is a strange one—never was there a human being more dependent for happiness on domestic affection than myself—and scarcely one to whom it has been more denied."

In 1849, Mantell described a new dinosaur. On a trip to Lewes, he bought a 54-inch-long (137-cm-long) humerus (upper foreleg bone) from the town miller. He was sure it did not belong to an *Iguanodon* or to any of the known kinds of dinosaur. Mantell had discovered the first sauropod, a type of giant dinosaur marked by its long neck, long tail, thick legs, and heavy body. He named it *Pelorosaurus*, meaning "monstrously gigantic." Mantell had now identified three of the dozen known dinosaurs.

In 1848, nearly thirty years after the discovery of the *Iguanodon*, Mantell finally got his hands on a bone he had hoped to find, an *Iguanodon* jawbone complete with two immature teeth. Mantell's paper on the jawbone won a medal from the Geological Society in spite of the opposition of Richard Owen, an influential anatomist and paleontologist. Owen's attempt to prevent Mantell from winning the medal was part of a feud that blighted the last years of Mantell's life.

Owen is an important figure in the history of paleontology; he first introduced the term "dinosaur." Like Mantell, he had trained to be a surgeon, but instead of going into practice, he landed a teaching job at the Hunterian Museum of the Royal College of Surgeons. Here Owen studied comparative anatomy and became known as "the English Cuvier." Owen was the first to recognize that huge prehistoric animals found by Buckland and Mantell were not really lizards. Owen created a new category or "order" for them, which he named *Dinosauria*.

Over the years, Owen and Mantell seemed to have a cordial relationship, sharing bones, drawings, and information with one another. Nonetheless, these two personalities were often working on the same fossils in a very small field. Eventually they came into conflict, writing contradictory papers about some small marine fossils. Owen was basking in honors and hated to be contradicted, while Mantell was striving for recognition and determined not to be overlooked. The reading of Mantell's paper in a Royal Society meeting led to a public showdown. This tense meeting ended with Mantell's triumph, but Mantell left knowing he had made a powerful and spiteful enemy.

Still, despite these frustrations, new fossils never failed to delight him. In June 1852, he received some big blocks of stone from a spot in the Wealden where imprints of insect wings and legs had been discovered. An excited Mantell realized that these little creatures had "buzzed about the ears of the Iguanodon!" He writes, "I hunted with my microscope till two o'clock, and so went to bed by daylight. I caught nothing—not even a flea—but I enjoyed my musings notwithstanding."

One night that autumn, Mantell felt very ill and tired after giving a lecture. He crawled down the hall to his bedroom, but once he was in bed, he couldn't sleep. He took a strong dose of opiates to kill his pain. A servant sat with him until he fell asleep. Mantell never awoke. He died at about three o'clock the next afternoon on November 11, 1852.

Mantell's dispute with Sir Richard Owen almost cost him a medal from the Geological Society. Owen, pictured here, coined the term "dinosaur."

Mantell had requested that no one be invited to his funeral, so just a handful of people, including his engraver, his lawyer, and his cook, stood by to see him buried beside the grave of his daughter Hannah. The only family member present was his daughter Ellen.

In his will, Mantell directed that his spine be kept in the Hunterian Museum for surgeons to see. All his life Mantell had shown such energy in pursuing his interests that his constant complaints about his back probably grew tiresome to those around him. When his spine was examined, doctors found that his lower backbone was twisted and curved about three inches to the left. The hard swelling in his back was actually his displaced spine. Mantell's pain had been very real.

During his life, Mantell made a constant effort to popularize his discoveries. It was Mantell who coined the phrase "Age of Reptiles" in a magazine article. His books and his lectures were aimed not at an audience of specialists but at the general public. In one of his books, Mantell explains why the study of fossils was worth so much effort. He writes, "It is indeed within the power of every intelligent reader, by assiduity and perseverance, to attain the high privilege of those who walk in the midst of wonders, in circumstances where the uninformed and uninquiring eye can perceive neither novelty nor beauty." Mantell's fossils led to the discovery of a true world of wonders, a lush, tropical prehistoric world teeming with giant reptiles that once existed on the English downs.

3

"Bones for the Millions"

O. C. Marsh vs. Edward Drinker Cope in the Great Dinosaur Rush

In 1877, some bulky packages slowly journeyed east from the little town of Morrison, Colorado, to the two greatest American fossil collectors of their day. One shipment was addressed to the Yale office of Professor Othniel Charles Marsh. The other headed to the Philadelphia house of naturalist and collector Edward Drinker Cope. Both shipments contained fossil bones—huge ones that must have belonged to animals 50 to 60 feet (15.2 to 18.3 m) long.

The men who originally excavated the bones weren't sure what kind of animal they belonged to, but Marsh and Cope knew right away. They were dinosaur bones. Not too many kinds of dinosaurs had been identified in 1877. Most of them were known from only a few bones and bone fragments.

Both Cope and Marsh realized that nothing like these huge bones had ever turned up anywhere else on earth. It was literally the biggest discovery in the history of dinosaur paleontology up to that time. It was also the beginning of a North American dinosaur bone bonanza. For the next fifteen years, the American West would prove to have some of the richest dinosaur fossil beds in the world. The finds came fast; Cope and Marsh raced each other to them.

In the scientific world, the first person to publish a scientific description of a new creature gets the honor of naming it. Less than a month after receiving his bones from Morrison, Marsh rushed into print with a description of "a new and gigantic dinosaur," the biggest land animal ever discovered. Marsh had described a new species of sauropod. He named his species *Atlantosaurus montanus*. A month later, Cope topped Marsh by describing an even bigger sauropod, *Camarasaurus supremus*.

Both Cope and Marsh immediately hired bands of bone collectors. Each team uncovered thousands of pounds of bones. In fact, both men now had more work than either one would be able to complete in his lifetime. In the midst of all this plenty, Cope and Marsh begrudged one another every new bone. Each one tried to keep the other from finding out where his men were digging. One of Marsh's best collectors, John Bell Hatcher, wrote, "I think the idea of keeping a corner on fossils of any kind should be given up. . . . But if . . . Cope or any one else see fit to send collectors into this rich field (which they have a right to do) there are bones here for the millions and it would be the utmost folly for me to attempt to keep them from getting some of them."

Over his lifetime, Marsh won the race for new dinosaurs; in all, he identified eighty new species to Cope's fifty-six. Both also found hundreds of new prehistoric reptiles, fish, birds, and mammals. Here Cope pulled ahead. Overall Marsh described 496 new vertebrates and Cope a dazzling 1,115. Between the two of them, they filled in the life history of past epochs, added whole branches to the tree of life, and enriched their own lives with successful exploration and scientific contributions. Yet through all this superabundance of fossils and fulfillment, each kept an anxious, jealous eye on the other.

It hadn't always been this way; in fact, the two men started out as friends. In 1868, at the beginning of their careers, the two went fossil hunting together near Haddonfield, New

In the race to find bigger and bigger sauropods, Cope discovered the Camarasaurus supremus, *shown here.*

Jersey. Marsh was thirty-seven years old and Cope, twenty-eight. Both were accepted members of the scientific community. They shared an interest in paleontology and a great love of the outdoors. The greenish sands around Haddonfield preserved fossils of the large Cretaceous reptiles called mosasaurs. Cope found ten species; Marsh found seven and named one *Mosasaurus copeanus* after his friend.

It seemed as if Cope had always known what he wanted to do. Cope was born on July 28, 1840, to a wealthy Quaker family. The Copes lived near Philadelphia on an eight-acre (3.2-hectare) farm called "Fairfield." Cope's mother died when he was only three years old, but his upbringing was always full of affection—from relatives, from a good-hearted stepmother, and especially from his father, Alfred Cope.

Alfred Cope gave his son the run of his gardens, fields, and his excellent home library.

From the age of six, Edward recorded things that interested him. One early journal entry describes a 114-foot-long (34.7-meter-long) fossil sea serpent that he saw in a Philadelphia museum. No one realized at the time that the serpent was actually several fossil whale skeletons strung together. Early in his life, Cope became an expert on American reptiles and amphibians. At age fourteen, Cope's father sent him to work summers on different farms. As he learned farming, Cope continued learning about the natural world. In one letter, he counts thirty-one species of willow trees in the neighborhood. In another, he reports finding a rare burrowing swallow. At eighteen, Cope enrolled at the University of Pennsylvania in Philadelphia to study comparative anatomy. At nineteen, he published his first scientific paper, describing two new species of salamander. At twenty, Cope traveled to Europe, where he studied museum collections and met the eminent European scientists of his day.

In 1864, Cope came home. He married a cousin named Annie Pim, and in 1866 their daughter Julia was born. Cope had admired Annie for her "amiability . . . as well as her steady seriousness." The many letters Cope wrote to both his wife and his daughter, reveal the closeness of their family. Cope was given a farm by his father, but he sold it to support his fossil hunting expeditions. Thanks to his family's wealth, Cope was free to do the work of his own choosing.

Cope had once written from the Smithsonian in Washington, D.C., "I can learn something every second, & am getting perfectly ravenous." If Cope was ravenous and quick, Marsh was persistent and tenacious. His childhood had been hard and narrow without the opportunities open to Cope. Othniel Charles Marsh was born on October 29, 1831. Like Cope, he was the oldest child, and his mother, Mary

Edward Drinker Cope

Peabody Marsh, died when he was three. His father remarried and settled his growing family on a small farm in Lockport, New York. The Marshes struggled to make ends meet. As the oldest of six siblings and half-siblings, Othniel had a burdensome round of chores and farmwork. The only time for schooling was in winter, after the harvest.

When Othniel was fourteen, a neighbor interested him in fossil hunting. Lockport offered excellent fossil hunting because the Erie Canal passed close by. Digging the canal channel had exposed a rock layer called the Rochester shale, which teemed with the fossils of sea plants and prehistoric sea creatures called trilobites. Marsh had a good eye for spotting fossils and the collector's instinct to hold on to them. In his diary, he wrote down a rule for himself, "Never part with a good mineral until you have a better." He followed his own rule. Some of the trilobites he found as a young man were still in his collection thirty years later.

At twenty, Marsh was uncertain what to do in life. He thought of perhaps becoming a carpenter. When he inherited some money from his mother's estate, however, he decided to go away to school, even though he knew he would be years older than all the other students. During this time, his mother's family, the Peabodys, stepped in and changed Marsh's prospects in life completely. Marsh's uncle, George Peabody, had made a fortune in banking. In spite of his great success, Peabody always regretted his own lack of education. When Marsh was ready to go to college, Peabody agreed to pay for his nephew's college education at Yale.

In New Haven, Connecticut, Marsh rented a third floor apartment and filled it with rocks and fossils until his landlord had to strengthen the sagging floor. Marsh lived well for a student. His classmates called him "Captain," and O. C. replaced Othniel in his signature. Marsh's ambitions had changed; he no longer had any notion of being a carpenter.

Othniel Charles Marsh

Now he aspired to become a Yale professor. Peabody encouraged him and supported him through three years of graduate study at Yale, and three more years in Germany.

At the time, Yale was expanding its science offerings. In Marsh, they had an excellent and hardworking student backed by an enormously wealthy uncle. When Marsh began asking about a possible professorship, his teachers suggested paleontology. No university in the country had a professor of paleontology, and Yale had only a few fossils. But the University administration had a hunch that, with Peabody backing him, Marsh would be able to bring a fossil collection in with him.

At Marsh's urging, Peabody donated the money to erect a new building, the Peabody Museum, for the university in 1863. In 1866, Yale offered Marsh a professorship, but the appointment came with no salary! Marsh accepted. He didn't need the salary; his uncle provided an annual income. Moreover, no salary meant no teaching. Marsh was free to arrange things to suit himself.

What suited Marsh was fossil hunting out West. Marsh had a talent for organization. He got a group of Yale students who could pay their own way and hooked up with an escort of U.S. Army troops to protect his group from hostile American Indians. They rode the railroad west to North Platte, Nebraska, and then switched to Indian ponies to roam regions of the West inaccessible by rail. His first expedition, in 1870, traveled with six wagonloads of provisions and an escort of forty-three soldiers.

Marsh thrived on expedition life, chipping away at fossils during the day, hunting buffalo for dinner, and telling tales around the campfire at night. In 1874, Marsh even risked his life for some fossils. The American Indian tribes in the area would not believe Marsh wasn't after gold. Working quickly, he and his collecting crew excavated fossils until they received a warning that a war party was looking for them. Marsh delayed one more day to pack his fossils securely so the bumpy wagon ride would not destroy them. He narrowly escaped the war party. The Indians named him Big Bone Chief.

On his yearly expeditions, Marsh was finding wonderful material all over the West. In 1872, Cope decided to go west, too. To Marsh's dismay, Cope turned up in the same area as Marsh, the Uinta Basin of Wyoming. Marsh did not want any other paleontologist horning in on a place he considered his digging grounds, especially not Cope. Cope, for his part, relished the West. He wrote letters to his wife and daughter describing prairie flowers as tall as a man, herds of buffalo racing alongside his train, and rattlesnakes that his ponies trampled under foot. In one letter he writes, "Marsh has been doing a great deal I find, but has left more for me."

Cope spent his days digging out fossils and his evenings dreaming up new names for them. He was able to identify a new species from very slight evidence—a few teeth, a jawbone, a legbone. Marsh could too, but he liked to proceed carefully. Marsh preferred to spend the winter studying new fossils, comparing them to the bones in his collections, and finally, making his identifications. Cope didn't have the patience. He studied his fossil finds around the campfire at night and then telegraphed in his discoveries to make sure he named them before Marsh.

All through the hot, dusty summer, Cope and Marsh rode through narrow ravines, checking the stone walls for pieces of bone and slowly chiseling fossils out of the rocks. After each discovery, they had to wonder if their rival had already found such a fossil and taken credit for it. The fiercest battle was over the *Uintatherium*, a 6-foot-tall (1.8-meter-tall), barrel-bodied mammal with three pairs of horns on its head. In 1872, Both Cope and Marsh uncovered the bones of many of these big mammals. Cope rushed to take credit for seven different species. Marsh disputed Cope's claims; he had already named some of the same animals. Between the two of them, they generated a confusing jumble of names and claims. One thing was clear—their friendship was over.

In the 1870s, the United States government sponsored several surveys. Their goal was to explore the geology, geography, and resources of the western territories. For a number of years, Cope worked for the U.S. Geological Survey. There was no salary, but the government did pay his expenses and publish his findings. On one survey trip in 1874, Cope made one of his most spectacular finds: a deposit of very early, very rare Eocene mammals in New Mexico.

When he couldn't hook up with a survey, Cope funded his own expeditions. On an 1876 expedition in the Judith River basin of Montana, Cope found *Monoclonius crassus*, a dinosaur with three horns—one on its nose and one over each eye. This dinosaur, a relative of *Triceratops*, was the first member of the ceratopsian group ever discovered. Hunting in the Judith River badlands proved difficult. Along with his companion, Charles Sternberg, Cope dug for fossils on steep, crumbly ravines. Their cook and their game hunter deserted out of fear of the warring Sioux Indians. When it came time to pack up and take home 1,700 pounds (771 kg) of bones, Cope and Sternberg had to lower the wagonload of fossils down the cliff with ropes. Despite the obstacles, Cope considered it a very good trip. He had found eighteen new dinosaurs.

Marsh's financial backing allowed him to hire collectors to work for him. Some of them were simply diggers; others were trained scientists. From all of them, Marsh demanded that they scour each location to get skeletons as complete as possible. Sometimes his crews spent months sifting through rubble, looking for missing pieces of bone. He could afford to be thorough.

A dispute over naming new species of this prehistoric mammal, the Uintatherium, *inflamed the feud between Cope and Marsh.*

In 1873, one of Marsh's collectors sent him a mixed box of bones. As he studied these bones, Marsh gradually realized that he had one of the most important finds of his life. The bones came from a prehistoric diving bird with teeth. No one had ever found a bird with teeth before. This bird was one of the missing links between reptiles and birds. Marsh named it *Hesperornis regalis* and sent his collectors after more of them. By 1880, Marsh had bones from 125 of these birds.

After 1874, Marsh's growing fossil collection at Yale kept him so busy that he no longer spent his summers in the field. Still, when Marsh took an interest in a fossil, he insisted that his hired collectors find as many as possible. After John Bell Hatcher sent him his first *Triceratops* skull, Marsh wanted more. Over the next three years, Hatcher provided thirty-one huge skulls, each one about 6 feet (1.8 m) long.

In the years since their clash in 1872, Cope and Marsh had gone different ways, each collecting different creatures in different quarries. But when the huge sauropods lumbered into their lives in 1877, the sheer size of the discoveries could not be ignored. The race was back on. At first it looked as if Cope had won. One of Marsh's diggers wrote from Colorado, "I am very sorry to find that Cope is getting by far the best lot of fossils. Where we are at work the sandstone renders the bones less accessible and when uncovered they are so extremely friable and broken that it seems almost useless to send them."

Then Marsh received a letter about a place in Colorado called Como Bluff. This fossil bed turned out to be even richer than Cope's quarry and easier to work. In 1879, Marsh's collectors dug out an almost complete sauropod skeleton. Marsh named it *Brontosaurus excelsus*. He didn't realize that he had already named this species *Apatosaurus* two years earlier. Officially, the scientific name is *Apatosaurus*, but *Brontosaurus*, meaning "thunder lizard," is most popular.

Always a thorough scientist, Marsh directed his collectors
to find as many Triceratops skulls as possible.

Other dinosaurs first discovered at Como include *Stegosaurus*,
with its row of armor plates, the carnivore *Allosaurus*, and a
small dinosaur named *Nanosaurus*.

In the fall of 1879, the United States government reor-
ganized the U.S. Geological Survey. Unfortunately for Cope,
the new head was a Yale man and friend of Marsh named
Clarence King. King appointed Marsh the survey's official
Vertebrate Paleontologist. With this appointment Marsh
could afford to have several crews working in the field, while
keeping preparators, illustrators, and researchers busy at

Yale. Over the next ten years, Marsh employed more than fifty people.

Cope, on the other hand, lost his position in the survey. Congress had promised to publish Cope's survey work, and in 1885 the government did publish a one-thousand-page volume containing Cope's descriptions of 350 Cenozoic animals. Cope had enough material for a second volume. He had done the fieldwork, studied the fossils, and written the descriptions. Now he wanted the government to publish it. But Congress insisted that printing his first huge work had used up all the money available for the project. During the next decade, Cope would spend many weary hours in various Washington waiting rooms trying to get a grant for the second volume.

In 1878, Cope bought a publication called *The American Naturalist*. With his own journal, Cope could now publish even faster than Marsh, but he had to spend a great deal of money to keep *The Naturalist* afloat. During the 1880s, Cope did not have a great deal of money. Cope needed a job, but he couldn't find one. He invested his remaining money in silver mines and lost most of it. Without any institutional backing or government appointment, Cope could not do the extensive fieldwork he had done in the 1870s.

Cope occupied a pair of houses right next to each other on Pine Street in Philadelphia. He lived in one and made the other his office and museum. The first floor of his museum overflowed with boxes of fossils. On the second floor, Cope set up more fossils all around his office. The pages of *The American Naturalist*, ready for editing, cluttered his desk. In a corner stood a cot that Cope slept on when his family was away. A terrarium housed a gila monster, and a big tortoise wandered around the room. His one employee, a preparator, worked on the third floor. From this cramped office, Cope wrote articles and prepared lectures, but he was galled by the success and influence of his rival, Marsh.

Marsh mistakenly named this dinosaur twice: Apatosaurus *the first time and* Brontosaurus *the second. Its scientific name is* Apatosaurus, *but it is still widely known as the* Brontosaurus.

Marsh lived in an eighteen-room house built on 7 acres (2.8 hectares) of land in New Haven. He later added a greenhouse that he filled with more than 1,300 rare orchids. Marsh collected art, too, and he packed his house with beautiful objects. Sometimes his friends joked that he never married because he would have wanted a collection of wives. Now the most influential paleontologist in the country, Marsh commanded one of the biggest fossil collections in the world.

Brilliant men came to work for Marsh because at Yale they could work with fossil material available nowhere else.

But many of Marsh's employees were very unhappy with their boss. In the first place, Marsh was unreliable about paying regularly. Maybe because he didn't lack money himself, he didn't seem to understand how important a regular paycheck could be. This particularly exasperated his field collectors. One collector, John Bell Hatcher, reported wading through an icy river to get to a little Texas town where he expected to find the paycheck he needed to sustain his fossil dig. There was no check; Marsh had not sent it.

On top of this, Marsh considered all his collections to be his and only his intellectual property. He hired trained scientists to make comparative studies of the fossils, but he didn't want any of his assistants publishing their own work. He habitually refused to share credit with them for the articles they worked on. These frustrated and angry men found that there was someone who understood their complaints and was always ready to hear them—Cope.

In 1889, Cope had begun teaching at the University of Pennsylvania in Philadelphia. The Geological Survey still refused to print the second volume of his work. Cope didn't believe money was the reason. He suspected that Marsh was blocking publication in order to steal the credit. Then in 1889, he received a letter telling him to turn over all his fossils to the government since they had been collected as part of the survey. Cope was outraged. He had gotten no salary for his years in the field and had spent about $75,000 on his collection. The fossils clearly belonged to Cope, not the government. On January 12, 1890, he retaliated.

Cope put together his long list of complaints against Marsh and added the accusations he had gathered from Marsh's unhappy assistants. He gave the whole story to a *New York Herald* reporter who wrote it up as sensationally as he could. The headline blared out, "Scientists Wage Bitter Warfare . . . Allegations of Ignorance, Plagiarism and Incompetence . . . Lots of Hard Nuts Provided for Scientific Digestion—Will Congress Investigate?" The article accused Marsh of keeping survey fossils for himself; of concealing his fossils from other paleontologists; and of taking credit for works actually written by his assistants. The next week, Marsh answered the accusations and struck back with a list of every error Cope had ever made. Marsh had this to say about Cope's attack, "He has devoted some of his best years to its preparation . . . and it may thus be regarded as the crowning work of his life."

This fight became a national scandal. It forced scientists all over the country to take sides and nearly lost Cope his job. Marsh seemed to get away ruffled, but undamaged. It turned out that he had kept detailed records of just what fossils belonged to the government and what to him. Cope kept up the fight against Marsh in his own *American Naturalist*. In a private letter, he wrote, "Either he or I must go under. He should be compelled to retire, or at least I should not be crushed if I am right."

Marsh was not forced to retire, but neither was Cope crushed. In 1892, Cope was asked to do fieldwork for the Texas Geological Survey. At the age of fifty-two years, Cope jumped at the offer. On his way home, Cope made a detour to South Dakota. There his Sioux guide led him to a place where "the ground was covered with fragments of Dinosaurs, small and large . . . at the hill were numerous bones of giants nearly entire; one could hardly walk without stepping on them." Cope had found the Laramie formation.

In 1892, Marsh's fortunes also changed. Congress had made deep cuts in the survey budget. After ten years as the survey's official Vertebrate Paleontologist, Marsh received a telegram, "Appropriation cut off. Please send your resignation at once." This came at a time when Marsh's money was running out. Marsh had to close down most of his field operations.

In 1895, Cope sold his collection of fossil mammals to

Marsh and Cope discovered many of the best known
dinosaurs including the carnivorous Allosaurus.

the American Museum of Natural History in New York. The
museum paid thirty-two thousand dollars for the fossils of
10,000 individual animals belonging to 463 different
species. Cope estimated that these fossils amounted to only
two-fifths of his collection. In the winter of 1897, Cope
became ill. He wrote to his daughter that he preferred stay-
ing at his office because, "I can work between the times
when I have pain." On April 12, 1897, lying on his cot
amidst his papers, books, and fossils, Cope died. His funer-

al was at Fairfield, his childhood home. But Cope was not buried there, or anywhere. He gave his body to science, directing in his will that his brain and his skeleton be preserved for study. His skeleton is still at the University of Pennsylvania where it has been proposed as the type specimen for *Homo sapiens*.

Marsh survived Cope by only a few years. In 1898, Marsh formally gave his vast collection to Yale University as a gift. Like Cope, Marsh worked right up to the very end of his life. In the winter of 1899, he walked home in a heavy rain and got wet and cold. A few days later, Marsh went home sick and never returned to the Peabody Museum. He died of pneumonia in his home on March 18, 1899 and was buried in Yale's cemetery plot. His tombstone reads, "To Yale he gave his collections, his services, and his estate."

During their lives, Cope and Marsh set the pace for a tremendous expansion of dinosaur paleontology. When they began fossil hunting, nine dinosaur species had been discovered in North America. By the end of their lives, Marsh and Cope combined had found fifteen times that many. Their work resulted in better understanding of more dinosaur species than ever before. Many of today's best-known dinosaurs were their discoveries. Their finds and their rivalry fueled a surge of public interest which, in turn, helped support a surge of fossil hunting expeditions and dinosaur exhibitions. When Cope and Marsh began hunting dinosaurs, paleontology was an occupation for the independently wealthy. They left it an established field with career positions in universities and museums. Because of their tireless work in the rich fossil fields of the American West, their names have become as immortal as the fossils they uncovered.

4

"Bigger and Better Eggs"

Roy Chapman Andrews, Walter Granger, and the Fossil Fields of Mongolia

• •

Roy Chapman Andrews had to get out of the Mongolian Desert before winter came. Andrews and his second-in-command, paleontologist Walter Granger, had led a team from the American Museum of Natural History in New York to the Gobi Desert of Mongolia to search for traces of ancient man. The New York newspapers had christened it the "Missing Link" expedition. After a summer of searching, the Missing Link was still missing. Africa, not Central Asia, would prove to be the home of earliest man. But they had made other unexpected and amazing discoveries. Before the expedition, a single rhinoceros tooth was the only fossil ever found in Mongolia. But soon the Gobi was relinquishing some of the richest deposits of dinosaurs in the world. Fossil beds that Andrews' expedition located in the 1920s are still yielding new discoveries today.

Granger located the first dinosaur fossil in April on their fifth day out. He was still finding new deposits late in August. With no time to excavate, all Granger could do was map the deposits and hope to come back. On September 1, 1922, time was up. New snow blanketed the mountains and the colder nights warned of the coming winter. Early blizzards would turn the gravelly ground into a thick mud impossible for cars to drive through.

The Flaming Cliffs

The expedition's caravan of cars snaked its way east, out of the desert. At one stop, the expedition photographer, J. B. Shackelford, noticed a strange reddish ridge. He hurried over, promising that if he didn't find any fossils in five minutes, he would head right back. From the top of the ridge, he looked down a steep slope dotted with fossil bones. In a few minutes, he had picked up a complete skull, about eight inches long, lying right out in the open. The expedition drove no further that day. As Andrews described that after-

Roy Chapman Andrews poses with dinosaur eggs.

noon, "The badlands were almost paved with white fossil bones and all represented animals unknown to any of us." Sunset turned the sandstone cliffs a glowing red, so the expedition named the area the Flaming Cliffs. (It is now known as Bain-Dzak.)

No one in the group could identify the skull that Shackelford had found. They sent it on to the museum and got back an excited message. The skull belonged to a primitive ceratopsian dinosaur, a 9-foot-long (2.7-meter-long) relative of *Triceratops* with a similar beak and a smaller version of the neck frill. In honor of Andrews, the new dinosaur was named *Protoceratops andrewsi*, "Andrews's first-horned-face." *Protoceratops* caused great excitement in the world of paleontology, but the finds they made the following season would cause a worldwide sensation.

The next year, in April 1923, Andrews and Granger led the caravan back to the Flaming Cliffs. The second day, paleontology assistant George Olsen found three oval eggs exposed on the surface with two more rounded ends just showing. They looked like stony loaves of French bread embedded in Cretaceous rock. They were dinosaur eggs. Although paleontologists had always guessed that dinosaurs laid eggs, no one had ever found a dinosaur nest before. These hundred-million-year-old eggs made Andrews and his expedition famous.

With the slogan, "Bigger and better eggs," the expedition returned to the Flaming Cliffs one last time in 1925. They found forty more eggs: "Nests of them, singles, whole ones, broken eggs, big ones and little ones; eggs with smooth, paper thin shells, eggs with thick striated shells. In short, more eggs, different kinds and bigger and better eggs than any we had found."

Granger and Andrews tentatively matched the most common type of eggs with the most common fossil species, *Protoceratops andrewsi*. Now this identification is no longer

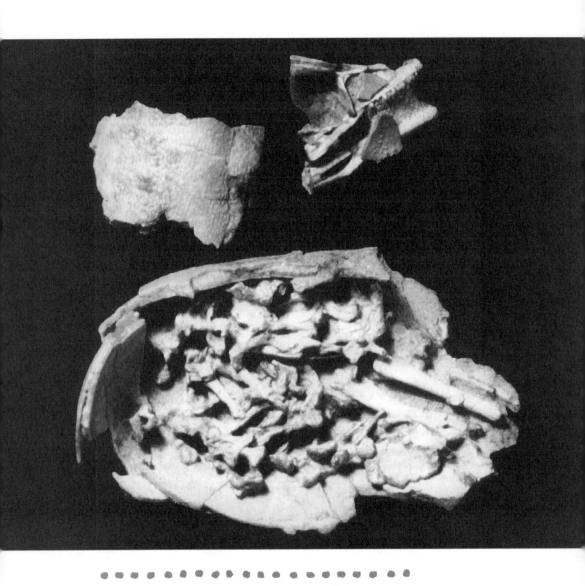

This egg containing an Oviraptor *embryo indicates that some of the eggs found in the Gobi previously thought to be* Protoceratops *eggs belong to other dinosour species. Paleontologists have not yet found evidence linking any of the eggs to the* Protoceratops.

accepted. Some of the eggs Andrews and Granger found may indeed belong to *Protoceratops,* but there is as yet no definitive proof. The only way to link an egg type with a dinosaur species is to find an egg with an embryo still inside. Fossil embryos are very, very rare. A fossil embryo found in the Gobi in 1993 shows that some of the eggs Andrews and Granger had linked to *Protoceratops* actually belonged to an 8-foot-long (2.4-meter-long) predatory dinosaur that the Andrews expedition had named *Oviraptor.*

In 1923, the expedition had picked up seventy-five *Protoceratops* skulls. In all, they recovered bones from more than one hundred *Protoceratops* individuals. At that time, no fossil bed had yielded the remains of so many individuals of the same species. What was even more unusual was that the bones belonged to animals of all ages, from tiny hatchlings to adults. For the first time, paleontologists could study how dinosaurs grew up. The fossil material they recovered is so rich that there is even rarer evidence of differences between males and females. One group of skulls has a higher flare to its neck frills and a more pronounced bony nasal bump. These skulls probably belonged to male dinosaurs.

But the eggs grabbed the headlines. At the end of the 1923 season, Andrews returned to New York to raise money. Everywhere he went, reporters clamored for news about the eggs. Like the great organizer he was, Andrews made the best of it. He held an egg auction. Newspapers around the world carried the story: one dinosaur egg would go to the highest bidder. Bids flooded in. So did donations. The egg finally went to Colgate University for $5,000, and all the publicity brought in ten times that much.

Andrews knew he needed more. He was a dashing figure, a confident optimist, and a great talker. Wiry and energetic, Andrews satisfied people's notions of how an explorer should look and act. He loved hunting exotic animals, and he played polo for relaxation. Field photos show him wear-

Andrews in the field

ing a broad brimmed hat, khakis, and riding boots, usually with a rifle in hand.

Although not himself wealthy, Andrews' growing reputation allowed him to mingle with wealthy people. He sometimes remarked on what charming people powerful financiers could be. In turn, Andrews charmed his wealthy friends into backing him with large donations. He convinced the Dodge Corporation to supply a new fleet of cars and Standard Oil to donate 20,000 gallons (75,708 l) of gasoline. Andrews sailed back to China with more than three hundred thousand dollars.

Andrews always had a gift for creating opportunities. He was born in Beloit, Wisconsin on January 26, 1884. As a young boy, he loved hunting and taught himself taxidermy. He later wrote, "From the time that I can remember anything I always intended to be an explorer, to work in a natural history museum, and to live out of doors. . . . Of course, I didn't know *how* I was going to do it, but I never let ways and means clutter my youthful dreams." The week after Andrews graduated from Beloit College, he went to New York City and asked for a job, any job, at the American Museum of Natural History. He was hired to mop floors for forty dollars a week. Andrews was thrilled.

By the time Andrews started at the American Museum, Walter Granger had been working there for sixteen years. Born on November 7, 1872 in Middletown Springs, Vermont, Walter displayed a love of nature from his youth. In an attempt to get Walter a job at the American Museum of Natural History, Granger's father contacted a friend there who headed the Department of Taxidermy. His friend let them know that if Walter could be there the next day, he could have a job. Granger arrived in New York City on October 1, 1890 to start work. He had completed two years of high school. His job included skinning animals in the taxidermy lab and cleaning and filling a row of outdoor kerosene lamps.

Granger's break came when the museum sent him west to collect mammal specimens in 1894. Granger loved fieldwork. His rugged and persistent nature suited him for the work, and his easygoing temperament and wry humor made him a great companion on these summerlong camping trips. Granger transferred into the Department of Vertebrate Paleontology in 1896 and worked in that department the rest of his life.

In 1897, the American Museum sent Granger on the first of six expeditions to Como Bluff, Wyoming, to search for Jurassic dinosaur bones. Henry Fairfield Osborn, then head of the Department of Vertebrate Paleontology, wanted a huge dinosaur skeleton to draw crowds to the museum. The second summer, Granger and some others came upon an unusual sheepherder's cabin made entirely of fossil bones. Whoever built Bone Cabin hadn't had to dig for the bones. They were scattered plentifully on the hillside. The Bone Cabin Quarry would yield 60,000 pounds (27,216 kg) of Jurassic dinosaur bones in one year alone. Among the fossils was an *Apatosaurus* skeleton, just the kind Osborn desired.

In 1903, Granger began a new field assignment in the Bridger Basin of Wyoming. He was searching for mammals from the Cenozoic period, which occurred just after the extinction of the dinosaurs. Without any formal education in paleontology or geology, Granger was able to learn so much in the field that his work mapping the layers of rock in the western fossil beds, and defining what fossils are found in each layer, is still standard. Matching particular fossils to particular rock layers, or strata, is called biostratigraphy. This study provides a history of prehistoric life because fossil species found in top layers lived more recently than those found in lower strata. Granger established the succession, or order, of strata in these western fossil beds, exposing evidence of the evolution and extinction of mammal species.

Back in New York, Granger married Anna Dean on

Granger and two other collectors unearth an Apatosaurus
fossil at Bone Cabin Quarry.

April 7, 1904, and settled into an apartment in Manhattan.
The couple had no children. By the time Andrews joined
the museum in 1906, Granger had developed into a great
collector with a sure sense of where bones should be and
vast patience in digging them out.

Andrews got his chance when he was sent to Long Island to retrieve the skeleton of a beached whale. He stood for days in icy water, digging bones out of wet sand, but he recovered a complete skeleton. Andrews talked the museum into sending him to a whaling station to study whales. Unfortunately, he made most of his observations while clinging weakly to the side of the ship between bouts of seasickness. Nevertheless, he returned with the first photographs ever taken of living whales.

Throughout his life, Andrews had a knack for choosing projects that had both scientific value and popular appeal. His next idea came from Henry Fairfield Osborn, now president of the museum. Osborn had a theory that human life originated in Central Asia. Andrews was eager to test Osborn's theory. Western scientists had not yet explored Central Asia, and Andrews knew that the results could be spectacular. Andrews wanted to start in the Yunnan Province of China, collecting zoological specimens. From this vantage point, he would scout an itinerary for a Central Asian Expedition. Osborn was all for it.

Yunnan shares borders with Laos and North Vietnam to the south and Tibet to the north. In the north, Andrews climbed 14,000 feet (4,267 m) up Snow Mountain to hunt the goral, a kind of mountain deer. Going southward, he camped for ten days in the tropical Salween Valley, one of the world's worst spots for malaria. In spite of the heat, Andrews and his men covered themselves completely with gloves, long sleeves, long pants tucked into boots, and mosquito netting over their heads. The only man to be bitten was Andrews himself. He lost his gloves, and mosquitoes bit his hands while he waited by the river for peacocks.

By the time Andrews emerged from the jungle, World War I had broken out in Europe. He managed to transport his collection of rare animal specimens back to New York. On October 7, 1914, he married Yvette Borup, the sister of an arctic explorer. Although they had two sons, George Borup and Roy Kevin, Andrews did not lead the life of a settled family man. When she could, Yvette Andrews joined her husband. She accompanied him on one scouting trip when they were almost eaten by wild Mongolian dogs, and she later went to the Mongolian capital with him to photograph traditional costumes. Their marriage, however, did not survive the decade of Central Asiatic Expeditions. The two divorced in 1931.

Near the end of the war, Andrews journeyed to Washington, D.C., hoping to work for the government. He secured an assignment that could not have been better chosen for him. The Navy instructed him to gather intelligence in Peking, China. This assignment gave Andrews the opportunity he needed to travel in Central Asia, learning its customs and studying the terrain. Twice he had to cross the Gobi Desert from Kalgan, a Chinese city near the Mongolian border, to Urga, the capital of Mongolia. For centuries, the only way to cross the Gobi was by camel. Although no paved roads or railroads spanned the desert, the big flat pads of camels' feet, crossing and recrossing the desert, had pounded the sand and mud into hard trails. Andrews realized that these trails were hard enough to support cars.

A camel caravan could reach Urga in two months. A car could do it in seven days. In 1918, however, a car was a rarity in Central Asia. The network of gas stations and paved roads that promoted automobile travel in the United States simply didn't exist in Mongolia. Nevertheless, Andrews made two car trips to Urga. It wasn't easy driving; the going was bumpy and cars often got mired in sand or mud.

One trip had to be made in winter. Andrews ran the engine constantly to prevent it from freezing. In the open car, the cold wind buffeted him for all 650 miles (1,046 km). That's how Andrews learned that fieldwork in Mongolia could only take place between April and September. Despite these difficulties, Andrews was excited about using cars. It would mean less travel time and more time for fieldwork.

During his trip, Andrews had a chance to experience firsthand the dangers and political chaos in Mongolia. Violent revolutions gripped both China to the south and Russia to the north. Factions from both countries used Mongolia as a battleground. Because of Mongolia's strategic position, China, Russia, and the rising Pacific power, Japan, wanted to control it. Andrews would have to deal with Chinese, Mongolian, and Russian authorities to get safely in and out of the country. And no authority could provide protection in the Mongolian heartland where both bandits and soldiers preyed on travelers. Nevertheless, the more he thought about it, the more Andrews was drawn to Mongolia. After the war, he returned to New York and told Osborn, "Mongolia is the place."

Daring as he was, Andrews was also a careful planner. He loved to quote an explorer friend who said, "Adventures are a mark of incompetence." When asked by newspaper reporters what hardships he expected to encounter, Andrews answered, none. He spent his time in New York raising money and purchasing eighteen tons of supplies. When his men came back to base camp from a hot, dusty day in the Gobi, they would not have to crouch around a campfire and eat out of cans. The expedition would have a cook with a portable oven and a pantry of dried fruits and vegetables to work with. The desert herds of wild gazelle and antelope would furnish the main dishes. The men would sit in folding chairs at a field table that would be covered with a tablecloth. As Andrews said, "I don't believe in hardships; they are a great nuisance. . . . Eat well, sleep well and dress well, then one can work well!"

Andrews knew that cars couldn't possibly carry all the men, equipment, food, and gasoline for an entire season. He solved this problem by acquiring a support caravan of 150

Andrews' use of cars contributed to the success of
the Central Asiatic Expeditions. On the far left stands
photographer J. B. Shackelford; Andrews
stands in the center.

camels. The camels met up with the cars at set points. The men would then unload the food, and fill the boxes with fossils for the camels to carry back.

To make the most of the field season, Andrews assembled a group of specialists to pool their knowledge. This was a new approach to scientific exploration. He commissioned topographers to map the country and geologists to figure out its stratigraphy; paleontologists and paleobotanists to search out and study its fossils; zoologists, including himself, to collect animal specimens; and a photographer to film and photograph the entire effort. Andrews chose his men carefully. Granger was an easy choice for second-in-command. The two of them would work together in Asia for the next ten years.

In spite of all Andrews' provisions against hardship, the expedition did go through some trying ordeals. With only a few minute's warning, fast-moving windstorms would whirl through the camp, covering everyone with a dense cloud of stinging, suffocating grit. Ironically, the expedition owed a lot to these sandstorms. Back in Cretaceous times, sandstorms just like these had buried and perfectly preserved the fossils they were finding.

The men of the expedition had to take care not to become fossils themselves. In July 1925, a violent storm ripped through the area at dawn. In fifteen minutes, the storm sucked clothes, dishes, chairs, and tents into the cloud and scattered the debris half a mile (0.8 km) across the desert. Granger threw himself across a suitcase to hold it down. It held perhaps the rarest fossils he had found, six skulls of Cretaceous mammals, each about 1.5 inches (3.8 cm) long. Granger had chipped through thousands of balls of rock, called concretions, to find these tiny fossils. These little shrew-like creatures had lived alongside the dinosaurs at the Flaming Cliffs.

Andrews always said that once Granger started looking for fossils, he didn't miss much. Andrews valued Granger's

Andrews surveys his support caravan of camels.

patience with fossils because he didn't have it himself. Always ambitious for the big finds, Andrews liked to cover lots of ground. He seemed happiest racing a car full-out to clock a running herd of gazelles or maneuvering the car to keep up with a wild ass so Shackelford could film it on the run. Andrews did find fossils, but when he found them he was always tempted to go at them with a pickax.

In 1922, Andrews located some fossil teeth that looked promising, but as he chiseled out the fossils, they crumbled to powder. Andrews knew he had better turn the job over to Granger. Granger spent four days working with a small brush, gum arabic, and damp rice-paper to cement the fossil together, bit by bit. As he revealed the fossil, he realized that the rock contained not just teeth, but a huge skull fragment. They identified it as a species of *Baluchitherium*, the largest land mammal that ever lived. It stood 13 feet (4 m) high at the shoulder and had a head 5 feet (1.5 m) long. Osborn rewarded Granger's work by naming it *Baluchitherium grangeri*.

Later, American Museum paleontologists realized that Russian scientists had already named this species *Indricotherium transouralicum*. So, this huge mammal is no longer named after Granger, but the skull that Granger excavated is still on exhibit in the museum.

In 1925, they located the lower bones of an *Indricotherium*'s right hind leg set upright in a hillside. This puzzled Granger; fossils are almost never preserved standing up. He guessed that the animal sank in quicksand, and he figured that an *Indricotherium*'s foreleg would have to be about three yards from its back leg. He was right. He soon had the lower fragments of all four legs. Looking over the wonderful find, Andrews said, "Walter, what do you mean by getting only the legs?" "It is your fault," Granger answered, "Why didn't you bring us here thirty-five thousand years earlier before that hill weathered away?"

As the years passed, Andrews and Granger kept finding more and more valuable fossil material in the Gobi. At the same time, the prospects for continuing their work became more uncertain with every year. They had become accustomed to confronting bandits and dodging random gunfire. But the wars and politics of the region made all the official arrangements difficult and uncertain. Throughout China,

Walter Granger was renowned for his patience and
care in excavating and restoring fossils. Here, he prepares
a protoceratops for exhibition in the American
Museum of Natural History.

hostility against foreigners mounted as the Chinese threw off foreign control.

In 1925, Mongolian officials arrested the camel caravan and detained it for three months. In 1927, the expedition's plans were "all shot to pieces," as Andrews put it, by war in China. In 1928, the expedition got into Mongolia, but authorities confiscated their fossils and accused the expedition members of spying. Andrews had come to regret the great egg auction because it convinced Chinese authorities that all fossils would command similarly high prices. In 1930, the last expedition was allowed into Mongolia, but they had to follow many restrictions, including making no maps. Andrews wrote, "Our whole plan of operations was crippled. It simply wasn't good enough. I decided to quit even though we had only scratched the surface of the Gobi."

The end of the Central Asiatic Expeditions marked a big change in both Andrews' and Granger's lives. Granger returned to New York in 1931. The collection of fossils they had been shipping back from the Gobi for a decade was waiting for him. The museum gave Granger a new title, Curator of Paleontology in the Department of Asiatic Exploration and Research. He now had the huge job of overseeing the preparation, study, publication, and exhibition of their Central Asian material.

For years, Andrews figured he would go back to the Gobi when conditions were right, but he was never able to do so. After the final expedition, he undertook writing the story of the expedition. He chose to do his writing in China, away from the social life and lecture demands of New York. Every day he rose at 3 P.M., lunched, and played polo. This ritual relaxed him enough to write until about 3 A.M. He finished his book, *The New Conquest of Asia*, in 1932.

When the director of the museum fell ill in 1934, Andrews agreed to fill the job for six months. At the end of six months, the museum invited him to keep the job.

Andrews accepted. Shortly after accepting the job, Andrews married a widow named Wilhelmina Christmas Butler. They settled in a two-story Manhattan apartment filled with furnishings Andrews had brought back from China. City living didn't agree with Andrews. He said, "In twenty years of exploration I have experienced at most 20 narrow escapes, or less than one a year. I challenge any urban resident suffering the perils of street traffic, subway travel and other city dangers to equal this record."

Andrews had taken the museum job at a difficult time, right in the middle of the Depression. Money was scarce. Big projects, started in more prosperous days, stalled for lack of funds to finish them. The museum depended heavily on Andrews' fund-raising skills. He invited potential donors to elegant dinner parties in the museum and publicized the museum on radio programs. The museum staff scrimped on supplies, and Andrews looked for budget cuts. But Andrews couldn't bear laying off men whom he had worked with and admired for years. When faced with this task in 1942, he resigned from the museum.

During Andrews' years as director, Granger worked hard on the Central Asian collection. Granger did not get a chance to lead any more field expeditions, but every summer, he used his vacation to lend a hand in whatever fossil dig the museum had going. In 1941, he traveled to the Big Badlands of South Dakota to collect with one of his best friends, preparator Bill Thomson. During this trip, on September 6, 1941, Walter Granger died in his sleep. Paleontologist George Gaylord Simpson wrote in a memorial, "It can seldom be said of a man of outstanding position, a man who was strong and determined and who would not recognize defeat, that he never made an enemy, but this can truthfully be said of Walter Granger. He had no acquaintances: everyone who knew him was his friend. . . . His infectious laugh dominated all gatherings. He had inexhaustible zest and he enjoyed life to the full, every minute of it, whether he was laughing at imminent death in windswept wilds or was laughing at a rollicking party in Greenwich Village."

Roy Chapman Andrews survived Granger by nearly twenty years. When he left the museum, Andrews retired to a small Connecticut property, called Pondwood Farm. He and his wife refinished a farmhouse, stocked their pond with bass and trout, and built a small, secluded log cabin where Andrews did his writing. In the winter of 1943, Andrews found himself snowed in with a broken leg. He used this winter of confinement to write his autobiography. The title, *Under a Lucky Star*, summed up his attitude toward life.

In 1959, Andrews authored his last book, a children's book called *In the Days of the Dinosaurs*. He died of a heart attack in Carmel, California, on March 11, 1960. Possessing the energy and the personality to make paleontology exciting to the public, Andrews was the prototype of the celebrity-paleontologist and a real-life Indiana Jones. His large-scale, team approach to exploring became a model for later expeditions.

The Mongolian fossil fields have continued to attract paleontologists ever since Andrews' expeditions. In the late 1940s, Russian scientists found a trove of Cretaceous dinosaur fossils in Mongolia. In the 1960s, Mongolian scientists teamed up with Polish paleontologists under the leadership of Zofia Kielan-Jaworowska to dig out a series of nearly complete dinosaur skeletons. In the 1990s, the American Museum of Natural History continues to send teams into the Gobi.

In 1993, an American Museum team found a skeleton that sheds new light on *Oviraptor*. When Andrews' men found the first *Oviraptor* skeleton just above the first dinosaur nest they encountered at the Flaming Cliffs, they concluded that the birdlike dinosaur had been caught in the act of stealing some *Protoceratops* eggs. They gave the supposed thief the Latin name meaning "egg-stealer." In 1993,

In 1993, new fossil evidence indicated that the Oviraptor *was actually a nurturing parent. This drawing shows an* Oviraptor *defending its nest.*

the American Museum paleontologists realized that the *Oviraptor* had actually been protecting its own nest. They found an *Oviraptor* skeleton crouched like a brooding bird over a nest of fifteen fossil eggs—another first for the Gobi. Fossil discoveries are likely to keep coming from Mongolia, all because in the 1920s Andrews and Granger gambled on the Gobi. Their gamble is still paying off.

"A New Theory, a Heresy."

Robert Bakker and the Dinosaur Success Story

Robert Bakker began his career as a dinosaur heretic by taking a long hard look at dinosaur elbows. Born on March 24, 1945, his fascination with dinosaurs began when he was a 10-year-old boy growing up in Ridgewood, New Jersey. At ten, he came across a dinosaur article with great illustrations in *Life* magazine. From that time on, Bakker devoted himself to dinosaurs. The closest dinosaur bones resided in the American Museum of Natural History in New York. Whenever he could get there, Bakker spent his time with the dinosaurs on the fourth floor. His parents and his older brother waited for him to outgrow his love for dinosaurs, but in the mid-1960s he was still studying them as an undergraduate at Yale University.

In Yale's Peabody Museum, he came face to face with a *Centrosaurus* that simply looked wrong to him. *Centrosaurus* is a relative of *Triceratops*; it has a neck frill with one big horn centered over its nose and smaller horns over each eye socket. This particular skeleton had been standing there for a little more than thirty years, and no one had found fault with it. But when Robert Bakker looked at this skeleton he couldn't believe that any animal ever walked the earth on such mismatched legs. The back legs came straight down from its hip sockets, but the forelegs were bent with the elbows stuck out to the side as if the centrosaur were trying to do a push-up. This brought the dinosaur's immense head down lower than its hips. To Bakker, it looked like the centrosaur had the front legs of a lizard and the back legs of a rhino.

He investigated. He found lots of justifications for the bent forelegs, but none of them satisfied him. Under all the explanations lay an assumption that Bakker didn't accept. Because dinosaurs are extinct, the explanations implied, they must have been evolutionary failures. Features such as the stegosaur's plates, the centrosaur's big neck frill, the brontosaur's huge size and tiny head—all of these were accepted as evolutionary excesses, just more evidence showing why these fascinating but outlandish animals didn't survive.

Bakker didn't envision dinosaurs that way. From his point of view, dinosaurs were incredibly successful. During most of their existence, they ruled the world. They were plentiful and adaptable. Dinosaurs lived on every land mass, and wherever they lived they occupied the top niches—the biggest plant eaters and the biggest meat eaters were dinosaurs. Bakker writes, "No nondinosaur larger than a modern turkey walked the land during the Age of Dinosaurs." And the Age of Dinosaurs was 160 million years long.

This attitude, that dinosaurs are a great success story, is what got Bakker started as a heretic. If he viewed dinosaurs as successful animals, then their bodies, their bones, had to make sense. In fact, their most outlandish features—beaks, crests, plates, frills, or sheer mass—had to be practical adaptations.

In his junior year at Yale, Bakker was named a Scholar of the House. Instead of going to classes, he could give all his time to one big project—the centrosaur's forelegs. Bakker approached the problem from several different angles. First, he examined some living animals who have splayed-out forelegs—lizards and alligators.

Studying living animals is an approach he recommends to anyone interested in dinosaurs. Before you look at a bone, he says, "Go to the zoo and take a video camera. Film animals walking and chewing and fighting and grooming." After that, "Dissect!" Bakker still remembers cutting into a pickled shark and marveling at its gills: "All those delicate fibers. It was beautiful. You can't understand nature without dissection."

Bakker persuaded his parents to buy him a movie camera. He bought some research subjects—a little menagerie of lizards and young alligators. Then he spent hours lying on his stomach, filming the lizards and alligators as they walked around the museum basement. Once in a while, he got great footage when an alligator charged right at the camera. Sometimes he waited a second too long and got nipped. After he filmed, he dissected.

He noticed something interesting. Alligator elbows do not stick out as far as lizard elbows; their legs are more upright. Bakker termed them semi-erect. In evolutionary history, the most primitive stance was the splayed, bent-elbow, lizardlike stance. Alligators evolved after lizards, and one of the things that distinguishes them from lizards is their semi-erect posture. Dinosaurs evolved later than lizards, too. Would it make sense that dinosaurs had evolved an advanced pair of erect back legs, but held on to the more primitive and lizardlike, splayed front legs? Bakker didn't think this had happened, but he needed evidence from the bones themselves.

According to Bakker, one of the best ways to learn about a bone is to draw it. "When you draw a bone, you're dissecting it with your mind. Drawing helps you to see what is really important: the places where muscles attach, the hollows, the joint surfaces." Bakker drew every dinosaur shoulder socket he could find in Yale's anatomy collection. In all his drawings, the hollow of dinosaur shoulder sockets faced down. This indicated that their legs did not swing out to the side like lizards, but forward and back under the dinosaurs' bodies.

Bakker looked at footprints to find additional proof for his theory. Wherever dinosaur tracks remain, the right and left footprints are not set wide apart but close together, near the body midline. The evidence supported the image of a centrosaur trotting along on two sets of upright legs. In 1968, Bakker wrote up his results in a paper called "The Superiority of Dinosaurs."

Bakker graduated from Yale during the Vietnam War years. While in college, he had not been eligible to be drafted into the army. But soon after graduation, he had to face the Ridgewood draft board. Bakker had grown up in a very religious family. He knew the Bible well, and although he did not accept the Bible as a scientific document, he did accept it as a religious one. In an hour-long argument, he convinced the draft board that his religious principles prohibited him from taking part in any war. The board granted him the status of conscientious objector.

In 1971, Bakker attended Harvard University to work on his doctorate at Harvard's Museum of Comparative Zoology. He addressed a question raised by his undergraduate research: which was more energy efficient, a walking lizard or a walking mammal? Bakker chose animals of the same size, fitted them with gas masks attached to an oxygen analyzer, and got them to move along on little treadmills.

He expected to find that the mammal with its erect legs used less energy than the sprawled out lizard. To his surprise, the data showed that exactly the opposite was true. Moving on erect legs used *more* energy. What advantage, then, did dinosaurs gain from the erect gait? Possibly the stance gave them greater speed. This propelled Bakker into the next investigation: how fast could dinosaurs run?

Part of his graduate work sent Bakker to South Africa where he did fieldwork in dinosaur fossil beds and studied African wildlife. On one occasion, seeing a white rhino run inspired him. Bakker writes, "I observed a three-ton white rhino bull at a full gallop with all four huge feet off the ground simultaneously in mid-stride. . . . Perhaps big quadrupedal dinosaurs could also quick-start off into their own clomping high-speed charge." This set him to measuring the length of dinosaur leg bones, looking at the angles of the joints, studying the muscle attachment sites on knees and thighs, calculating the weight-bearing strength of the bones, and figuring the range of motion of the shoulder blades. His conclusions again upset the standard image of dinosaurs as clumsy lumberers. In his opinion, a five-ton *Triceratops* could gallop along. He writes, "Speed and vigor were the way of the dinosaurs. . . . The Mesozoic was life in the behemoth fast lane."

Piece by piece, Bakker was assembling the evidence to support a big idea: that dinosaurs were warm-blooded, that is, they used energy generated by their metabolism to maintain a constant body temperature. Bakker believes that dinosaurs didn't live like dim, sluggish reptiles; their mammal-like metabolism allowed them to be as active as mammals. To prove this, Bakker has had to dispute many theories. Some scientists, for example, think dinosaurs lived in a warm climate that allowed them to grow quickly to very large sizes without having to spend much energy on keeping themselves warm. Others believe that the sheer size of some adult dinosaurs helps them to conserve body heat; they stay warm by being large—it's called gigantothermy. But how, Bakker wonders, would small, young dinosaurs regulate their body heat? Bakker does not believe that dinosaurs depended on the sun's heat or on a warm climate or on the heat-conserving mass of their own bodies. Bakker believes that dinosaurs maintained a constant body temperature; that they were able to compete with mammals and win out because they had a metabolism that could compete with a mammal's metabolism.

Bakker put his ideas forward in articles and at meetings during his graduate school years. Controversy followed. Bakker seemed to thrive on controversy. Even though he

Bakker believes dinosaurs were very active creatures. This new vision comes through in recent representations of dinosaur life, such as this dynamic scene of several triceratops fending of a tyrannosaur.

took his degrees from two of the most elite and prestigious universities in the country, Bakker nevertheless had a firm sense of himself as an intellectual outsider. His work has a feisty quality; he's not just recording data, he's looking for a fight. He writes, "When I began to publish reconstructions of galloping dinosaurs, the shrill voice of outraged orthodoxy rose to deafening heights."

Since his days at Yale, actually since his boyhood visits to the American Museum of Natural History, Bakker had been thinking about the *Apatosaurus* (which is the scientific name for the dinosaur commonly called *Brontosaurus*). The orthodox idea about the brontosaur was that it was too heavy to support its own weight, that it spent most of its life half submerged in swamps, eating soft water weeds. At Harvard, Bakker was part of a big project, the Morrison Dinosaur Habitat Research Group. Every summer, the group traveled to the Morrison fossil beds near Como, Wyoming. The Morrison formation is a layer of Jurassic mudstone rich in sauropod fossils. This layer of relatively soft, pastel-colored shale is named after the Colorado town of Morrison, but the formation is found in several western states. This is the formation where Cope and Marsh raced each other to discover bigger and bigger sauropods in the 1880s.

They dug a trench down 300 feet (91 m) through the entire Morrison layer. Their trench cut through twenty layers of fossils, exposing lots of evidence that conflicted with the traditional notion that brontosaurs lived in swamps. The research group found teeth of land-dwelling predators, such as *Allosaurus*, scattered among the brontosaur bones. Just as significant were the fossils they didn't find; no fossils of fish or turtles mixed in with the brontosaurs. If the Morrison brontosaurs had lived in lakes and swamps surely bones of lake and swamp creatures would have been preserved along with theirs. The evidence ruled out lakes and swamps as brontosaur habitats. In 1980, the group published its findings; brontosaurs lived on dry land.

By that time, Bakker had finished his Ph.D. and accepted a teaching job in the Department of Earth and Planetary Sciences of Johns Hopkins University in Baltimore, Maryland. There he taught comparative anatomy and led digs in

Bakker's work has helped dispel the notion of apatosaurs
living half submerged in swamps.

the summers. During these years, Bakker kept working on one dinosaur-related problem after another. Somehow, every dilemma the fossils presented seemed to lead back to the idea of warm-blooded dinosaurs. After eight years at Johns Hopkins, Bakker resigned and moved west to Boulder, Colorado. As he explains it, he wanted to be near the fossil beds. Two years later, in 1986, he collected his thoughts in a book, *The Dinosaur Heresies.*

The Dinosaur Heresies bristles with all kinds of ideas about all kinds of dinosaurs. Bakker drew all the illustrations for the book. He has never had any formal art training but he does have years of drawing experience. These illustrations, whether of bones or fleshed-out dinosaurs, have a precise kind of vigor. In one drawing, an adult *Diplodocus* swings its long neck to the left while it whips its tail to the right. *Diplodocus* is one of the big, long-necked, long-tailed sauropods. From the tip of its tail to the top of its neck, the *Diplodocus* spine forms an S-curve. It's not a sluggish pose; the move has momentum. In the drawing, the adult *Diplodocus* comes out swinging to keep two allosaurs away from its young one. Bakker sees even the massive sauropods as alert, active, and social. The image is backed by an array of research.

He counters the idea that a sauropod's tiny head and weak teeth couldn't process enough food to fuel much activity. First, he looks for a good comparison and comes up with the moa, an extinct New Zealand bird that also had a small head perched on a long slender neck.

Moas didn't chew their food up; they pulverized it in gizzards. A gizzard is a muscular, stomach-like organ lined with stones that the bird has swallowed. Dissection shows that crocodiles have gizzards, and so do ostriches and other birds. Why not sauropods? In his fieldwork, Bakker recalls seeing smooth pebbles strewn around *Apatosaurus* skeletons. If they were gizzard stones, it would certainly explain how these small-headed dinosaurs could process large amounts of food.

Bakker envisions even the large sauropods as relatively nimble creatures. He believes this diplodocus could use its tail as a defensive weapon.

He offers more thoughts on sauropod diets. He looks at the wear patterns on fossil teeth to conclude that the vegetation they cropped was definitely not swamp mush. He studied the way sauropod skulls and necks connect to decide whether the dinosaurs reached out or up for food. He speculates about brontosaur faces and lips and wonders whether past paleontologists were right when they suggested that *Diplodocus* may have had a trunk like an elephant.

How high could they graze? Three kinds of sauropod, including *Apatosaurus* and *Diplodocus* have short backs, tall spines on the vertebrae near their hips, and supple tails. With powerful back muscles attached to the vertebral spines, Bakker thinks they had enough leverage to rear up into a tripodal stance. Bakker envisions flocks of these sauropods rearing up on their hind legs, bracing themselves with their long tails, and stretching their long necks to feed on 30-foot-high (9-meter-high) vegetation.

Could any sauropod really rear up like that? Many paleontologists don't think so, but Bakker points out that he isn't the first one to suggest the tripodal feeding pose. O. C. Marsh suggested it for *Stegosaurus* a century before, and Elmer Riggs, a Chicago paleontologist, had worked it out for *Diplodocus* in 1904. To those who wonder how a sauropod heart could pump enough blood 40 feet (12 m) up to its brain, he notes that sauropods are very unusual because as they evolved, their brain cases actually got smaller. "There was virtually no brain to pump blood to!"

Statements like this are part of Bakker's style; in print and on the podium, he makes his ideas understandable and entertaining. Not one to hoard his thoughts, Bakker fires off a generous assortment of ideas and explanations. He is definite about what he thinks. Given a set of facts, Bakker will go out on a limb to connect them and express the connection in the strongest possible terms. It's paleontology with an attitude. The attitude may be what is bothering other paleontologists more than the ideas. And his shoot-from-the-hip style sometimes bypasses conventional scientific methodology.

Bakker's big idea, that dinosaurs were warm-blooded, is still controversial, too. Some paleontologists think he's right about some dinosaurs, but not all of them. Some think he's right about dinosaur lifestyle but wrong about how their metabolism worked. Bakker has certainly caused paleontologists everywhere to take another look at both fossils and assumptions.

In his attempt to prove that dinosaurs were warm-blooded, Bakker has incorporated a wide variety of scientific work

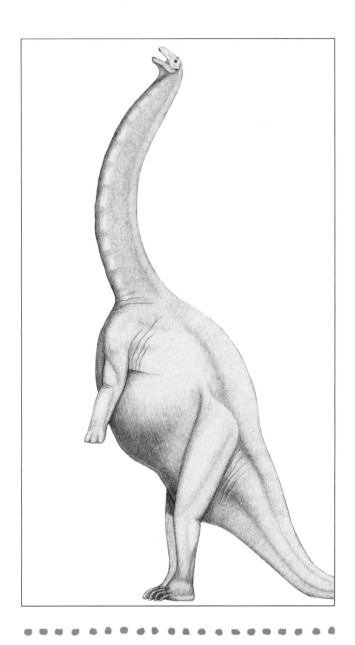

Bakker suggests that the Apatosaurus *could rear up into a tripodal position to feed on high vegetation.*

into his line of argument. He cites studies on dinosaur bone tissue that may indicate that young dinosaurs grew quickly, like birds or mammals, rather than slowly, like reptiles. He also ties in projections of the size and capacity of dinosaur digestive tracts. One of the key elements of his study is a measurement called the predator-to-prey ratio. This is a comparison between the number of meat-eating animals and the number of animals available for them to feed on. The ratio is not a simple head count; Bakker figures in each animal's body weight to get an idea of the pounds of meat available per each pound of predator. This is a useful technique because the ratio is very different for cold-blooded and warm-blooded predators. Cold-blooded predators don't eat as much or as often as warm-blooded ones. The same number of prey animals can support many more cold-blooded predators than warm-blooded ones.

After years of work, Bakker's results show that the ratio for dinosaurs is closer to the pattern for warm-blooded predators. There are few of them in comparison to their prey; for example, Bakker calculates that tyrannosaurs represented 3 to 5 percent of their prey populations. By other counts, the ratio of predatory dinosaurs to their prey is higher—up to 10 percent. Bakker notes that these ratios are higher than those for living mammal predators, such as African lions. Nevertheless, the ratio for dinosaurs still falls considerably short of the ratio typical for cold-blooded predators, which is 20 to 25 percent.

Despite this data, serious challenges to the warm-blooded dinosaur theory remain. Some hinge on dinosaur anatomy. For example, the nose area of the skulls of warm-blooded animals contain tiny scrolls of bone cartilage called respiratory turbinates. The turbinates help prevent loss of heat and moisture when an animal exhales. Most dinosaur skulls show no evidence of turbinates. Does this prove that they were cold-blooded? Another question focuses on the overall number of dinosaurs that inhabited given areas. Dinosaur populations were denser than those of modern mammals. Some paleontologists wonder how so many large animals could survive if they ate at a warm-blooded rate.

Questions like these keep Bakker and other paleontologists busy reexamining skulls and gathering data about the dinosaurs' environments. Whether the evidence ultimately supports or opposes Bakker's vision of dinosaurs, he has certainly had a hand in shaping the direction of research in paleontology today. His work has contributed to a major shift in paleontologists' thinking about dinosaurs. Thanks to new discoveries and to the work of paleontologists like Yale's John Ostrom, most paleontologists now believe that birds are the living descendants of dinosaurs. This cheers Bakker. Back in the 1970s he wanted to change the way dinosaurs were classified. He didn't think they belonged in the same class as reptiles. He would like to give them their own class with three major branches, one for the flying pterosaurs; one for all the herbivores, including sauropods, duckbills, and all the armored dinosaurs; and one for theropods, including carnivorous dinosaurs—such as allosaurs, tyrannosaurs, and oviraptors—as well as birds.

Since Bakker left Johns Hopkins in 1974, he has not taken another teaching job. His controversial views about dinosaurs have made him famous. Kids who fall in love with dinosaurs are likely to know who Bob Bakker is. Television specials about dinosaurs and paleontologists almost always include an appearance by Bakker. Sometimes he is shown at a dig; sometimes in a museum. Wherever he is shown, Bakker looks the part of a field paleontologist. He has on a cowboy hat to keep off the desert sun; a field vest with lots of pockets; and jeans and boots for rugged climbing. He wears his long brown hair in a ponytail and has a full, bushy beard. Whenever he appears, Bakker also manages to get across the excitement he feels about dinosaurs and the absolute conviction that his vision of them is right.

As a result, he is in great demand as a lecturer and a consultant on all kinds of dinosaur-related projects, from museum mounts to video games. Lecturing and consulting fees finance his continuing research and fieldwork. Fortunately, Bakker likes lecturing. He says, "It's all part of sharing the wealth. If you're fortunate enough to dig bones, share the intellectual wealth. Tell people why it's important. In return, you'll get questions that never occurred to you."

Bakker does hold a position as curator at the Tate Museum in Casper, Wyoming, but this post commands what he calls a "negative salary." That means that Bakker donates substantial portions of his earnings to the museum to support work in paleontology. To him, this is a time-honored arrangement. He cites other paleontologists who used their book royalties to fund research projects and pay student assistants. But Bakker is unusual among paleontologists because he is a kind of one-man institution of dinosaur studies. Paleontology-with-an-attitude has worked out well for him. The controversies he has raised have made him a celebrity. His celebrity status makes it possible for him to generate his own funding and follow his own research agenda.

Bakker goes out to a dig nearly every month. In the summers, he leads amateur fossil hunters into the field, and they almost always find some good fossils. "If you think you like paleontology, take a field course," Bakker says. When you get out there, he has some advice: "The key to fieldwork is to go real slow. Pay attention to everything. The most important thing is not to be looking for anything in particular. The most exciting discovery is one you don't expect."

On a recent dig near Como, Bakker believes his group made just such a find—something no one expected—an

A.M. No. 5753

Would an allosaur such as this one drag slabs of meat back to its nest? Bakker's research suggests this may have happened.

Allosaurus nest site. *Allosauruses* were Jurassic predators about 20 feet (6 m) long with big heads, big teeth, and little forelegs. They moved around on powerful back legs. No one had ever found a nest site for any of the big meat-eaters before. Bakker has found big 6-foot-long (1.8-meter-long) bones, grooved by *Allosaurus* teeth marks and surrounded by broken off teeth. Clearly, some allosaurs were chewing up a big carcass. What makes this find notable is that the allosaur teeth range from adult size to the tiny, tiny teeth of extremely young animals. Bakker estimates that the smallest teeth belonged to babies only a few days old.

When Bakker was ten years old, one tableau in New York's Museum of Natural History captivated him. In the scene, an *Allosaurus* crouches over an *Apatosaurus* carcass. The fossils came from Como. The tableau was mounted in 1910 and still stands in the museum, unchanged. Now, with his recent discovery, Bakker can envision a new scene. In his tableau, adult allosaurs drag huge slabs of meat to a nest where hatchlings join in the feast. It's an exciting scene. What's more, it fits with everything Bakker has been saying all along. All he needs to see is a grooved bone and a pile of teeth to bring it all alive.

6

"Embryos in the Eggs and Newborns in Their Nests"

John Horner and the "Good Mother Dinosaur"

In 1978, John Horner used his whole vacation for dinosaur hunting. He had a good idea of what he was looking for and where he might find it. He was searching for the bones of young dinosaurs. Fossils of baby or juvenile dinosaurs are extremely rare. Horner had thought a lot about why this should be; after all, young dinosaurs probably died in great numbers. Why had so few been found?

Horner was working as a fossil preparator for Princeton University. He had left his home state of Montana to take the Princeton job in New Jersey simply because he loved working with fossils. He had found quite a few dinosaur bones out in Montana, and he'd taken university courses in paleontology and geology. Now, his job gave him a chance to go behind the scenes and study fossil collections in many of the great museums in the eastern United States.

He had been to New York's American Museum of Natural History and seen the collection of *Protoceratops andrewsi* bones that Roy Chapman Andrews and his team brought back from Mongolia. The Mongolian *Protoceratops* bones came from animals of all ages—babies, juveniles, adults. In 1978, no other collection in the world could show such a complete record of the stages in a dinosaur's life. In fact, only a very few fossils of baby or juvenile dinosaurs of any kind had been found the world over.

Some duckbilled dinosaur bones in the Princeton collection started Horner wondering about young dinosaurs. The scientific name for the duckbilled dinosaurs is *Hadrosaurus*, which means "heavy lizard." Hadrosaurs possess a couple of distinctive traits. First, hadrosaurs are one of the only kinds of dinosaurs that could chew. They have rows of teeth on both their upper and lower jaws perfect for grinding foliage. Second, their skulls broaden out into a nose shaped something like a duck's bill. Some kinds of hadrosaurs have flat heads; some have bony crests, but all of them have a broad, flattened snout. In the late Cretaceous period, big herds of hadrosaurs roamed the American West. Today, hadrosaur fossils are not rare; in fact, their bones are some of the most commonly found dinosaur fossils in the American West. Perhaps that's why these particular bones in the Princeton collection had never been studied. They had never even been unwrapped.

As Horner studied these bones he saw something new about them, something that had been overlooked. Many of these bones had belonged to juvenile duckbills. The bones had been found in 1900, in a rock formation near Billings, Montana, called the Bear Paw shale. Horner thought this spot would be worth another look. Maybe he could find more juvenile fossils there. So in July 1978, that's where Horner and his fossil hunting buddy Bob Makela went for vacation. Just as they arrived, three solid days of rain turned the Bear Paw shale into mud. Horner only had a few weeks left before he had to go back to work. He couldn't afford to wait for the gluey mud to dry out and firm up, so he went to join another dig.

On the way, he stopped at a tiny rock shop in Bynum, Montana, because he heard they had some dinosaur fossils they couldn't identify. The owner showed Horner a collection of mysterious little bones and bone fragments she and her family had found. One was a piece of a thighbone about 1 inch (2.5 cm) long; another was a jawbone only 2 inches (5 cm) long. Horner knew duckbill bones when he saw them, and that's what these were. But they were so tiny. These had to be the bones of baby duckbills. Just by luck, Horner had found exactly what he was looking for.

The next day, Horner and Makela went out to look at the spot where these bones had been found. In the middle of a scrubby pasture on a Montana cattle ranch arose a stony bump. Pebbles and scraps of gray-black stone littered the top. Horner and Makela recognized these blackish scraps as fossils. They scraped the surface of the mound, collecting all the fossils they could find. When they sorted them out, they had bones belonging to two baby duckbilled dinosaurs.

Horner knew he had an important find, and he wanted to see what other fossils might lie in the pasture. He called his boss, Princeton paleontologist Don Baird. Baird told Horner to keep digging and sent some expense money. His vacation had turned into an official expedition.

Back at the site, Horner and Makela carefully dug out bagfuls of the greenish mudstone from the top of the bump. When they had dug down about 3 feet (0.9 m), they hit a layer of red mudstone. That's where the fossils trailed off. As he looked at it, Horner saw that they had dug a bowl about 6 feet (1.8 m) across and 3 feet (0.9 m) deep. It occurred to him that this bowl filled with small bones was not an accident. He had found a nest that a dinosaur had built millions of years ago. This find began a series of discoveries that would change the way people think about dinosaurs.

Horner and Makela spent the next six summers leading digs to this and other nearby sites. Over years of returning to the same site, Horner was able to study it more thoroughly than Andrews and Granger had been able to study the fossil beds in Mongolia. He discovered the bones of two new species of dinosaurs. However, his most important discoveries were not the species themselves, but all the things he learned about how these dinosaurs lived and acted. From his work, Horner could claim to have found not just the first dinosaur nests in North America but the first dinosaur nesting colony.

In the pasture where they found the first nest, they uncovered seven more nests just like it: bowl-shaped depressions holding fossil eggshell fragments and baby dinosaur bones. Merely finding the nests together, however, did not necessarily indicate that they formed a colony. After all, the nests could all have been made by different dinosaurs over many years. Horner had to show that all the nests were built the same year.

Horner looked to the geology of the region for clues. The nests had all been found in the same layer of sedimentary rock. About 8 inches (20 cm) below the nests, Horner noticed a layer of jagged, marble-sized rock nodules called caliche. Horner knew that a particular layer of caliche only forms while the surface soil above it is neither buried nor eroded away. The nodules continue to grow in size as long as the surface soil is preserved. Scientists can tell exactly how many years it takes to "grow" caliche nodules of any given size, and can therefore also tell how long the soil above it was the topmost layer, even if it has since been buried for millions of years. The caliche nodules under the nests Horner found took between five and ten years to form. This means that the layer of earth where the dinosaurs built their nests was the topmost layer of soil for ten years at the most before it was covered by other sediment.

Narrowing the time span to ten years when the nests are eighty million years old is amazing. But what if the nests had been made by one dinosaur that kept coming back to the same ground, building a new nest each year? To answer this argument, Horner looked at the spacing of the nests them-

Jack Horner has found hadrosaur eggs at several locations in the American West, including this one aptly named Egg Mountain.

selves. None of them overlapped. In fact, the eight were spaced pretty evenly, about 23 feet (7 m) apart. As Horner turned up more fossils, he realized that the adult dinosaurs were 20 to 23 feet (6 to 7 m) long. The nests left just enough room for the adults to maneuver between them. This convinced Horner that these dinosaurs nested together.

The bones he found in the nests told Horner even more. Horner's crews found fourteen duckbill nests in three different nesting grounds, including bones from thirty-one individual baby dinosaurs. Horner noticed several things. First, he rarely found complete eggs. Most of the nests contained crushed and broken fragments. Second, the baby dinosaurs in the nests were different sizes. The smallest ones measured about 14 inches (36 cm) long. The biggest were 3.5 feet (1 m) long. Third, the smallest ones showed no wear on their teeth. Horner concluded that they were very new hatchlings. The bigger ones had worn teeth. They had been eating for awhile—enough to more than double in size.

But this brought Horner to a puzzle. Why would he find 3.5-foot-long (1-meter-long) dinosaurs in the nest unless, like birds, they stayed there for awhile? That would explain why the eggs were so fragmented; the little dinosaurs trampled them underfoot. This idea led Horner to another conclusion; the adult dinosaurs must have been feeding their young in the nest until they grew big enough to fend for themselves. Horner and Makela gave these duckbills the name *Maiasaura peeblesorum*. The word *peeblesorum* acknowledged the Peebles family who owned the pasture containing the nests. The word *Maiasaura* means "good mother lizard" in Greek.

Horner's conclusions were revolutionary; no one had ever pictured dinosaurs as nurturing parents before. His work overturned old ideas about the capabilities of dinosaurs. The evidence for parental care is indirect; it involves some deductions and assumptions. New data may call Horner's deductions into question. But the information he has gathered from the maiasaur nesting ground has changed the way paleontologists think about dinosaurs and the things they look for in fossil beds. Now that Horner has pieced together the image of a dinosaur nesting colony, it will be easier to recognize another one.

Near the nesting site, Horner's expedition found more

A maiasaur nest in the Museum of the Rockies

evidence of how the maiasaurs lived. Scattered in different sites, they found mixed up bones of thousands of adult dinosaurs. Horner realized that all these sites made up one huge bone bed containing the jumbled bones of at least 10,000 maiasaurs. The maiasaurs seem to have gathered in huge herds. Horner's son, Jason, who was eight years old at the time, discovered part of this bone bed at a site he named

Nosecone. For many summers, Jason was a regular at the maiasaur dig. He had been fossil hunting with his father since he was four years old.

Jack Horner started fossil hunting as a young boy, too. Horner, whose given name is John, was born on June 15, 1946, in Shelby, Montana, where his father had a sand-and-gravel plant. At age six, Jack Horner found his first dinosaur fossil. He writes, "Ever since then I've been interested in dinosaurs. But not all dinosaurs. The bone I found was a duckbilled dinosaur, and it is duckbills that I spend most of my time looking for and thinking about." Jack Horner was a fast walker; he covered lots of ground fossil hunting all around Shelby. Then he spent hours cleaning and preparing his finds in his family's basement.

By the time he left for the University of Montana, he was an experienced fossil-hunter determined to become a paleontologist. But school had never been easy for him. Jack Horner had dyslexia, a learning disability that makes it hard to decipher numbers and letters. When a dyslexic person looks at a word, the letters sometimes flip-flop; they may appear reversed and out of order. In the 1960s and 1970s, dyslexia wasn't widely recognized or well understood. None of his teachers realized that he had this problem. Jack himself didn't know about dyslexia, but he knew that some of the university's required subjects, such as a foreign language, were nearly impossible for him to learn.

In 1965, he flunked out of college and was drafted into the U.S. Marines. The marines sent him to Vietnam for a year where he searched through jungles for enemy soldiers. After his tour of duty ended, Horner returned to the university to try for his degree again. He took every graduate and undergraduate course in geology, biology, and paleontology that the university offered, but he still couldn't complete all the degree requirements. In 1973, he gave up on finishing his degree and went home to Shelby.

For a while he worked for his father, driving a gravel truck, but he kept looking for a job in paleontology. In 1975, he landed a job as a fossil preparator for Princeton University in New Jersey. Horner enjoyed a great working relationship with his boss, Don Baird. Baird encouraged Horner to work on his own projects. For Horner, this meant working on duckbills.

Horner knew that the very first nearly complete dinosaur skeleton ever found anywhere had been a duckbill. The skeleton turned up in a quarry near Haddonfield, New Jersey, in 1858. Horner visited this site only to find that it lay under a housing development. When he visited the Philadelphia Academy of Sciences to see the skeleton, he learned that the bones had been misplaced—separated and lost somewhere in the jumbled backrooms of the Academy. Horner set himself the task of hunting down the bones and reassembling them. His restoration of this first North American dinosaur skeleton is now part of the Academy's permanent dinosaur exhibit.

Then Horner rediscovered the overlooked duckbill bones in the Princeton collection. These juvenile dinosaur fossils led him, by a roundabout way, to the maiasaur nest out in Montana. His work on the maiasaurs has made Horner one of the best known paleontologists in the world. If you watch television programs about paleontology, you've probably seen him. Horner is a tall man with a calm, thoughtful way of speaking. He has often been filmed for TV and covered in the press. Film director Steven Spielberg called on Horner for advice on the dinosaurs in the movie *Jurassic Park*. Museums all over the world invite him to come and speak. The University of Montana has awarded him a degree, an honorary doctorate.

Now Horner works as curator of Paleontology at the Museum of the Rockies, which is run by Montana State University in Bozeman, Montana. The museum's permanent dinosaur

Horner prefers fleshed-out dioramas to skeleton
displays. Here, he poses beside his maiasaur nest diorama
in the Museum of the Rockies.

exhibits feature Horner's discoveries. Horner doesn't like displaying skeletons. He thinks it's "a peculiar way to look at dinosaurs." Instead, the Museum of the Rockies has constructed a diorama of maiasaur nestlings being fed by a parent.

As wonderful as these discoveries are, it is Horner's method of working on them and his way of thinking about them that has helped him move from simply identifying bones to reconstructing an animal's behavior. According to Horner, fossil hunting hasn't changed much since the days of Cope and Marsh. "You just go out and look. What has changed is our expectation of data gathering. Because of the techniques we have, we expect to get more data from the field."

When Horner's crew starts on a fossil bed, they don't just dig in. First they measure off the site and use string and stakes to divide it into a grid of squares. Then, as the digging begins, they map each square to show where every bone is found. This attention to the lay of the bones has helped Horner and other scientists who worked on these sites figure out how the animals lived and died. For example, in the huge maiasaur bone bed, the skeletons were all torn apart, but most of the bones lined up in the same direction. Horner speculates that some time after the herd died, probably killed by the poisonous gases of a huge volcano, a powerful flood surged over the bones, breaking individual skeletons apart and lining the bones up with the water's flow.

Horner can also use techniques that were simply not available to earlier paleontologists. For example, Horner found one clutch of dinosaur eggs where the stony surface was wearing away, and the tiny bones inside were starting to stick out. These were not maiasaur eggs. Horner and his crew had found a nesting ground for a smaller dinosaur, which Horner named *Orodromeus makelai*, "Makela's mountain runner." *Orodromeus* was a 9-foot-long (2.7-meter-long), lightly built dinosaur. For some reason, the eggs in one *Orodromeus* nest had never hatched.

An artist's conception of the Orodromeus *embryo,*
based on Horner's CAT scan

Horner took the same first step anyone would: he
cracked an egg to make sure embryonic bones remained
inside. But he didn't crack all of them. He had the rest of the
eggs CAT-scanned. This sophisticated X-ray technique provided him with a precise, 3-D image of the contents of each
egg. In most of the eggs, the bones had collapsed in a heap,
but the CAT scan showed him one egg in which the skeleton
was still fully articulated, that is, all its bones were still fixed
in place. It would later take four years to clean this one egg,

but thanks to the CAT scan, Horner didn't have to wait four years to study it.

Questions raised by the maiasaur babies also led Horner to look at the bones themselves in a new way. He took a selection of maiasaur bones to the Paris-based laboratory of Armand de Ricqles, an expert in the microscopic study of fossil bone. This field is called paleohistology. Horner and Jill Peterson, a paleontology student who had worked on the maiasaur dig for several years, started by making slides. They used a saw to cut thin cross sections of dinosaur bone, glued them to glass slides, and then ground and polished them on a grinding wheel until the cross sections were thin enough to let the light shine through the bone slices. What were they looking for?

Horner had been thinking about the baby maiasaurs in the nest. If they stayed there until they had doubled in size, how long would that take? If a little dinosaur grew at the rate of a cold-blooded reptile, such as an alligator, it could take a year. But if it grew at the rate of a warm-blooded bird, it might only take a month or two. Were these dinosaurs warm-blooded? Horner believed the dinosaur bones might hold clues to how fast maiasaurs grew.

In the 1960s, Ricqles had found mammal-like bone tissue in some groups of dinosaurs. The bones had lots of blood vessels, which correlates to fast growth. This led Ricqles and paleontologist Robert Bakker to suggest that dinosaurs were warm-blooded. But many questions remain. The only way to compare growth rates for different animals is to chart an animal's growth against it's own final adult size. But what is the final adult size of an animal, such as a dinosaur or crocodile, that never stops growing? Horner learned the techniques of paleohistology and began researching these questions in Paris.

The Museum of the Rockies has since set up their own histology lab to conduct microscopic studies of dinosaur bone. It's the only lab like it in the United States. By studying slides and looking at the bones of the maiasaur herds, Horner now has an idea of just how fast baby maiasaurs grew. He believes they could grow from a 14-inch (36-cm) hatchling to a 3.5-foot (1-m) baby in a little under a month. A one-year-old maiasaur would be about 9 feet (2.7 m) long. If Horner's calculations are correct, maiasaurs grow up quickly, like warm-blooded animals.

But they are not exactly like warm-blooded animals. As researchers examine this issue in greater depth, they find that dinosaurs do not exactly follow the growth and metabolism patterns for warm-blooded or cold-blooded animals. Many paleontologists, including Horner, believe that dinosaurs deserve their own category. Horner writes, "These bone studies are the best evidence I know of that dinosaurs had their own special metabolic strategy, unlike anything we know about before or since dinosaurs."

The museum's histology lab has also been useful in studying bone slices from another big find, a nearly complete *Tyrannosaurus rex* skeleton. Whereas duckbill fossils are fairly common, fossils of *Tyrannosaurus rex* are very, very rare. No complete skeletons have ever turned up. Up until 1993, all the *T. rex* bones found came from about a dozen individual animals. And all of them were found in western North America. Horner did not find his museum's *T. rex*; a Montana ranch owner named Kathy Wankel first located it. She and her husband were fossil hunting in the Montana badlands when she found a ridge of bone. The more she dug around it, the more bone she unearthed. Finally she took some of the bones to the Museum of the Rockies where Jack Horner identified them as the shoulder and arm of a *T. rex*— the first *T. rex* arm bone ever found.

The *Tyrannosaurus rex* bones were embedded in a layer of hard sandstone on a hill near Jordan, Montana. This hill is part of the Hell Creek Formation, a layer of rock deposited

In 1990, Horner and a crew excavated a rare
T. rex *fossil. Here, a fleshed-out tyrannosaur chases another*
carnivorous dinosaur called an albertosaur.

between sixty-five and sixty-seven million years ago at the
end of the Cretaceous period. During this time, the *T. rex*
lived alongside large herds of triceratops and duckbilled
dinosaurs and an assortment of small mammals.

During the summer of 1990, Horner and a crew of sea-
soned volunteers and staff members from the Museum of
the Rockies dug up the Wankel *Tyrannosaurus.* The skeleton
was ninety percent complete—the most complete *T. rex*
found up to that time. Horner approached this dig in the
same thorough manner he had used when he worked on the
maiasaur fossil beds. At the General Electric lab in Cincin-

nati, Ohio, Horner located a CAT scan machine big enough to hold the 5-foot-long (1.5-meter-long) dinosaur skull. The CAT scan yielded fifty cross-section images per inch (per 2.5 cm) all along the big skull. Once all this information is entered in a computer, it will be possible to generate an image of the skull from any angle.

Horner has written several books about his work. He has recently published *Dinosaur Eggs and Babies* with Kenneth Carpenter and Karl S. Hirsch. *Digging Dinosaurs*, written with James Gorman, recounts his seven years of fieldwork on the dinosaur nesting grounds. *The Complete T. Rex*, written with Don Lessem, begins with the discovery of the Wankel *T. rex* and then tells all there is to know about this dinosaur.

In the nineteenth century, an all-around naturalist such as Edward Drinker Cope could make significant contributions in many fields. Now, paleontologists have to consult specialists in many fields. Horner, for example draws on the work of all kinds of specialists: fossil plant experts, geologists, sculptors and artists, ecologists, zoologists, and geochemists. Horner compares this growth of specialties to evolution itself, "As we get more people, we are adapting to narrower niches." In his books, Horner gives us a picture of the community of people who study dinosaur paleontology. Where it is useful, Horner describes the work of other paleontologists. Where the experts disagree, he presents all sides. He's on the lookout for creative thinking and sound research that he can apply to understanding dinosaurs. He's also willing to have others work on the fossil material he's found.

Horner explains his attitude, "My assumption is that we all want to know the answers. I can gather a certain interpretation from the data, but it might be wrong. If it is, I want to know it. I'm not afraid to be wrong. I have no secrets. I want to share with other people—their insights may help me. I want to know."

Horner's love of what he does comes through strongly in

all his books. His research now centers on how evolution works. He wants to get at the mechanism of evolution—not so much what creatures change into as how and why they change. The dinosaur that offers the best opportunity for this study is Horner's favorite, the duckbill. He is beginning by looking at how duckbill species changed over hundreds of thousands of years.

Duckbills have always been lucky for Horner, ever since he found that first bone. On the other hand, Horner worked hard to be ready for his good fortune. When asked if he has any advice for young people, he says, "Whatever you're interested in, particularly in the biological sciences, pursue it regardless of whether it appears that it's popular. People don't perceive science as being popular; they don't think it's going to be accepted. But you can make it accepted. You can make people want to read about it and learn about it. You can make it interesting just by going out and being interested yourself."

GEOLOGIC TIME SCALE

Time Scale (Figures in millions of years)	ERAS	Duration of Periods	PERIODS			DOMINANT ANIMAL LIFE
10 20 40 60	CENOZOIC		Quaternary		Recent Pleistocene	Man
		70	Tertiary	EPOCHS	Pliocene Miocene Oligocene Eocene Paleocene	Mammals
80 100	MESOZOIC	75	Cretaceous			Dinosaurs
150 200		55	Jurassic			
		35	Triassic			
250	PALEOZOIC	40	Permian			Primitive reptiles
300		35	Pennsylvanian			
350		40	Mississippian			Amphibians
		50	Devonian			Fishes
400		40	Silurian			
450 500		65	Ordovician			Invertebrates
550		65	Cambrian			
Figures in millions of years	PRECAMBRIAN	Figures in millions of years	1500 million years duration			Beginnings of life

Only during the last 500,000,000 years have plants and animals produced hard parts capable of being fossilized. Here is a simplified chart of that quarter of the earth's history.

A Note on the Geologic Time Scale

In the mid-ninteenth century, a British survey-
or named William Smith was employed build-
ing canals in England. Smith took an interest in the fossils
revealed while cutting through the rock layers. Smith already
knew the principle of superposition, which says that younger
layers of rock have been deposited on top of older ones. He
began to compare the fossils he found in different layers, and
he realized that different rock strata contained different
kinds of fossils. He started checking in different locations
and found that no matter what type of rock he found, the
sequence of fossil remains was the same. In other words, all
rock strata (layers) containing the same type of fossil
ammonites must have been deposited in the same time period. It was still not possible to say exactly how long ago that
time period was, but with Smith's insight, it became possible
to arrange layers of rock and their fossil contents in order
from youngest to oldest. It became possible to say that no
Tyrannosaurus rex ever saw a trilobite because trilobites were
extinct long before tyrannosaurs evolved.

The geologic time scale follows this organization from
most recent times at the top to most ancient times at the bottom. First it divides the past into four long periods of time
called eras: the Precambrian (beginnings of life); the Paleo-

zoic (ancient life); Mesozoic (intermediate life), and Ceno-zoic (recent life). The eras are marked off one from another by mass extinctions. For example, the end of the dinosaurs marks the end of the Mesozoic Era. The eras are further divided into shorter spans of time called periods. The division into periods also reflects the appearance and disappearance of different plant and animal fossils. The earliest dinosaur remains have been found in rock strata deposited during the Triassic period; the latest fossils have been found in strata deposited during the Cretaceous period. With the discovery of radioactivity in the early twentieth century, it became possible to assign dates to geologic time periods. Radioactive elements decay at fixed constant rates, so by measuring the by-products of radioactive decay in a given rock layer, scientists can tell how old that layer is. The dates on the geologic time scale are often given in "mya," which stands for "millions of years ago." Dinosaurs first appeared about 225 million years ago and died out 66 million years ago.

Selected Bilbliography

Works preceeded by an asterisk (*) are recommended for young readers.

General Works Consulted

*Colbert, Edwin H. *The Great Dinosaur Hunters and Their Discoveries.* New York: Dover Publications, 1984.

*Czerkas, Sylvia J. and Stephen A. Czerkas. *Dinosaurs: A Global View.* New York: Mallard Press, 1991.

*Lucas, Spencer G. *Dinosaurs: The Textbook.* Dubuque, Iowa: Wm. C. Brown Publishers, 1994.

*Rudwick, Martin J. S. *The Meaning of Fossils: Episodes in the History of Palaeontology.* Chicago, Ill.: University of Chicago Press, 1976.

Chapter 1

Appel, Toby A. *The Cuvier-Geoffroy Debate: French Biology in the Decades before Darwin.* New York: Oxford University Press, 1987.

Coleman, William. *Georges Cuvier Zoologist: A Study in the History of Evolution Theory.* Cambridge, Mass.: Harvard University Press, 1964.

Cuvier, Baron Georges. *Essay on the Theory of the Earth.* Trans. by Robert Jameson. 5th ed. London: T. Cadell, 1827.

Lee, Mrs. R. *Memoirs of Baron Cuvier.* London: Longman, Rees, Orme, Brown, Green, & Longman, 1833.

Outram, Dorinda. *Georges Cuvier: Vocation, Science and*

Authority in Post-Revolutionary France. Manchester, England: Manchester University Press, 1984.

Chapter 2

Mantell, Gideon Algernon. *The Journal of Gideon Mantell: Surgeon and Geologist.* Ed. by E. Cecil Curwen. New York: Oxford University Press, 1940.

Mantell, Gideon Algernon. *The Medals of Creation: First Lessons in Geology, The Study of Organic Remains.* 2 vols. 2nd ed. London: Henry G. Bohn, 1854.

Spokes, Sidney. *Gideon Algernon Mantell, LL.D., F.R.C.S., F.R.S., Surgeon and Geologist.* London: John Bale, Sons & Danielsson, Ltd., 1927.

Chapter 3

*Lanham, Url. *The Bone Hunters: The Heroic Age of Paleontology in the American West.* New York: Dover Publications, 1973.

Osborn, Henry Fairfield. *Cope: Master Naturalist.* Princeton, N.J.: Princeton University Press, 1931.

*Ostrom, John H. and John S. McIntosh. *Marsh's Dinosaurs: The Collections from Como Bluff.* New Haven: Yale University Press, 1966.

Schuchert, Charles and Clara Mai LeVene. *O. C. Marsh: Pioneer in Paleontology.* New Haven: Yale University Press, 1940.

Chapter 4

*Andrews, Roy Chapman. *On the Trail of Ancient Man: A Narrative of the Fieldwork of the Central Asiatic Expeditions.* New York: G. P. Putnam's Sons, 1926.

*Andrews, Roy Chapman. *Under a Lucky Star: A Lifetime of Adventure*. New York: Viking Press, 1943.

*Colbert, Edwin H. *William Diller Matthew: Paleontologist*. New York: Columbia University Press, 1992.

Chapter 5

*Bakker, Robert T. *The Dinosaur Heresies: New Theories Unlocking the Mystery of the Dinosaurs and Their Extinction*. New York: William Morrow and Co., 1986.

*Monmaney, Terence. "The Dinosaur Heretic." *New Yorker*. May 31, 1993. pp. 42–52.

Chapter 6

*Horner, John R. and Don Lessem. *The Complete T. Rex*. New York: Simon & Schuster, 1993.

*Horner, John R. and James Gorman. *Digging Dinosaurs*. New York: Workman, 1989.

Internet Resources

Due to the changeable nature of the Internet, sites appear and disappear very quickly. These resources offered useful information on dinosaur paleontology at the time of publication. Internet addresses must be entered with capital and lowercase letters exactly as they appear.

Yahoo!
http://www.yahoo.com
The *Yahoo!* directory of the World Wide Web is an excellent place to find Internet sites on any topic.

The American Museum of Natural History
http://www.amnh.org/
Visit Fossil Halls in the exhibits section of this site and see how far this New York City museum has come since it sent Andrews and Granger into the Gobi desert.

The Field Museum of Natural History Exhibits Page
http://www.bvis.uic.edu/museum/exhibits/Exhibits.html
Take a chronological tour through the Age of Reptiles at this museum's Web site.

The Hunterian Museum Dinosaur Exhibit
http://www.gla.ac.uk/Museum/HuntMus/dinosaur/
More than a century and a half after Gideon Mantell visited the fossil collection of this museum to identify an *Iguanodon* tooth, the Hunterian Museum now has a Web site. The

dinosaur exhibit includes fossil dinosaur teeth donated to the museum by Mantell.

Illinois State Geological Survey Dinosaur Links
http://denr1.igis.uiuc.edu/isgsroot/dinos/vertpaleo.html
This site at the University of Chicago lists dozens of links to dinosaur related sites.

Royal Tyrrell Museum Web Site
http://tyrrell.magtech.ab.ca/
All kinds of dinosaurs are profiled in the Virtual Tour section of this Canadian museum's Web site.

Smithsonian Institution National Museum of Natural History Exhibits
http://nmnhwww.si.edu/exhibits.html
Click on Dinosaur Hall and view photographs from the dinosaur exhibits at this Washington, D.C., museum.

Tate Geological Museum Home Page
http://www.cc.whecn.edu/tate\webpage.htm
This Wyoming museum offers a gallery of Robert Bakker's dinosaur drawings.

The University of California Museum of Paleontology at Berkeley
http://www.ucmp.berkeley.edu/diapsids/dinosaur.html
This exhibit, titled *The Dinosauria: Truth is Stranger than Fiction,* offers a fascinating and complete look at the dinosaurs. The site also provides links to other sites of interest.

Index